BEAUTY&DUTY

The Art and Business of Renaissance Marriage

Bowdoin College Museum of Art
Brunswick, Maine

The publication of *Beauty and Duty:*
The Art and Business of Renaissance Marriage
accompanies an exhibition of the same title
at the Bowdoin College Museum of Art from
March 27 through July 27, 2008.

Copyright © 2008 by Bowdoin College.
ISBN: 978-0-916606-40-4

Beauty and Duty: The Art and Business
of Renaissance Marriage is supported by grants
from the Samuel H. Kress Foundation, the
Robert Lehman Foundation, the Cowles Charitable
Trust, and the Fisher Charitable Foundation
of Maine. The Stevens L. Frost Endowment Fund
and the Sylvia E. Ross Fund, Bowdoin College
endowment funds for the support of the
Bowdoin College Museum of Art, provided
major funding.

BEAUTY & DUTY
The Art and Business of Renaissance Marriage

INTRODUCTION

IT IS PROBABLY UNLIKELY that 600 years from now a contemporary hope chest will be scrutinized for all that it can reveal about twenty-first-century American social customs and values. Yet artifacts can be eloquent transmitters of their cultural context, or "messengers from a distant age," as the Samuel H. Kress Foundation acknowledged in establishing its "Old Masters in Context" program. Recognizing that museum objects have been "unmoored" from their original historic setting, the foundation sought to advance public understanding of the larger cultural milieu within which objects had found their human meaning.

In response to a 2001 Kress Foundation call for proposals, Susan Wegner, associate professor of art at Bowdoin and a specialist in Italian Renaissance and Baroque art, proposed to organize an exhibition on Renaissance marriage. She chose as her point of departure one of several gifts from the Kress Foundation to Bowdoin in 1961, a painting on wood that had once served as the front panel of a fifteenth-century *cassone*, or bridal chest.

The Kress Foundation proceeded generously to provide both a Planning Grant for Professor Wegner's initial research, and subsequently an Implementation Grant for the organization of the exhibition. The Robert Lehman Foundation has graciously subsidized the publication of this catalogue.

Support from the Fisher Charitable Foundation and the Cowles Charitable Trust has been critical to the realization of the project, as have been the contributions of the Stevens L. Frost Endowment Fund and the Sylvia E. Ross Fund for Museum of Art programming.

Beauty and Duty takes place in the inaugural year of the recently transformed Bowdoin College Museum of Art. Our newly installed, state-of-the-art climate control now allows us to borrow works of art from museums and collectors around the country, thus expanding the context of our own collections. Our newly renovated galleries provide an elegant and appropriate framework for the display of materials as varied as paintings, medals, furniture, prints, and books.

I am very grateful to all of our lenders for their willingness to participate, and to Professor Wegner for her years of single-minded dedication to unpacking the many facets of marriage in Renaissance Florence and other northern Italian cities. Her contagious enthusiasm has persuaded speakers, scholars, and conservation specialists, as well as the musicians, poets, and chefs whose talents help us celebrate the opening of this exhibition, to join together in recreating the context of one of the signal events of the human experience.

Katy Kline
Director, Bowdoin College Museum of Art

ACKNOWLEDGMENTS

DEEP THANKS go to the many colleagues who contributed generously to this exhibition and publication. Katy Kline, the director of the Bowdoin College Museum of Art, started the project on its way in 2001, when she invited Bowdoin's Art History Division to collaborate with the Museum in proposing a project for the Samuel H. Kress Foundation's "Old Masters in Context" initiative. Our initial proposal was accepted, and over the next seven years Katy shouldered the work of co-lead organizer, sharing the load in writing grants, conquering budgets, securing loan objects, constantly refining the project to a coherent theme and a realistic scope, and tirelessly editing texts, all the while keeping enthusiasm bubbling for the project even through the many months of the major renovation and expansion of the Walker Art Building.

Great gratitude goes to Suzanne Bergeron for her essential help with the publication and to Eric Anderson whose eagle eyes caught many a slip; to José Ribas '76 and Peter Shellenberger who overcame Herculean challenges to install the exhibition; and to Alison Ferris, Michelle Henning, Kacy Karlen, Laura Latman, Liza Nelson, Diana Tuite, and Victoria Wilson for sharing their professional expertise, insight, and interest. Lucie Teegarden's meticulous care as editor and Judy Kohn's fine design made the text and shape of this publication more pleasing to the eye and mind.

Bowdoin colleagues from many spheres helped the project in crucial ways: Tony Antolini, David Becker, Ken Cardone, Linda Docherty, Mary Agnes Edsall, Jennifer Edwards, Pamela Fletcher, Susan Grover, Anne Haas, David Israel, Marianne Jordan, Susan Kaplan, Aaron Kitch, De-nin Lee, Richard Lindemann, Julie McGee, Dede Medlen, Clif Olds, Steve Perkinson, Nina Pleasants, Deb Puhl, Arielle Saiber, Delmar Small, Jennifer Snow, Cindy Stocks, Cara Martin-Tetreault, Wiebke Theodore, Kevin Travers, Katharine Watson, and all of the members of the Bowdoin Antiques and Artifacts Committee, and of the Facilities Management, Music, Theater and Dance, and Art departments who shared their creative energies and good advice. We owe special thanks to Ruth Bartlett, whose effervescent enthusiasm continues to inspire us.

Bowdoin students Natasha Camilo '06, Lili Mugnier '07, and Sandra Pomerantz '00 conducted original research on objects from the Bowdoin College Museum of Art collections now included in this exhibition, and Nate Morrow '09 worked hard to help design educational activities for the Web site accompanying the show.

Colleagues Stephen Bonadies, Jon Brandon, John Coffey, Linda Coit, Lisa G. Corrin, Judith Deane, Maria DePrano, Paul Greenhalgh, Saralyn Reece Hardy, Beth Holman, Cristiane Joost-Gaugier, Laurence Kanter, John Marciano,

8 Genetta McLean, Stephanie Miller, Dan Mills, Russell Panczenko, Maria Ruvoldt, Jay Satterfield, George Shackelford, Robert Simon, David Steele, Susan Fisher Sterling, and many others gave invaluable aid in facilitating the loans of precious and fragile Renaissance objects and in bringing this project to completion.

I give my special thanks to my husband, John Fischer, for his continued good humor, patience, and consistent support throughout this project.

We are most grateful to the foundations who so generously supported the research, publication, and exhibition: the Samuel H. Kress Foundation's "Old Masters in Context" Initiative; the Robert Lehman Foundation, the Cowles Charitable Trust, the Fisher Charitable Foundation of Maine, the Jasper Jacob Stahl Lectureship, Cristle Collins Judd and the Office of the Dean for Academic Affairs for the "Visual Culture in the 21st Century" project, the Fletcher Family Research Award, the Bowdoin College Research Fund, Bowdoin College Sabbatical Leave support, the Robert Lehman Lectureship, the Art History Division, and special funds from the Bowdoin College Museum of Art, the Stevens L. Frost Endowment Fund and the Sylvia E. Ross Fund.

Finally, we would like to express our sincere thanks to President Barry Mills and all of the Trustees, alumni, and friends of Bowdoin who have committed themselves to the flourishing of the arts at the College.

Susan E. Wegner
Associate Professor of Art History

Figure 1:
*Scenes from Boccaccio's "Il Ninfale
Fiesolano" (Story of the Nymphs of Fiesole)*

Recently proposed attribution to
Fra Angelico (Checklist 1)

UNPACKING THE RENAISSANCE MARRIAGE CHEST:
IDEAL IMAGES AND ACTUAL LIVES

by **Susan E. Wegner**

Detail, Figure 15:
Nuptiae (see page 37)

Curiosity about an Italian Renaissance tempera painting on wood in the collection of the Bowdoin College Museum of Art sparked this exhibition, *Beauty and Duty: The Art and Business of Renaissance Marriage*. The panel, depicting nymphs, goddesses, and a love-sick shepherd (Figure 1), interprets episodes from Giovanni Boccaccio's (1313–1375) epic poem, *Il Ninfale Fiesolano (The Nymphs of Fiesole)*. The painting originally decorated the front of an early fifteenth-century Florentine marriage chest (*cassone*) and raises many questions. What beliefs about the nature of men and women does it express? How is its theme connected to marriage? What part did *cassoni* play in the rituals and celebrations of a Renaissance wedding?

This exhibition and publication unpack some of the messages contained in the painting and the *cassone* that it decorated.

Cassoni were among the most distinctive objects made on the occasion of Renaissance weddings in Tuscany and northern Italy. The chests' painted exteriors and the intended contents of their interiors reveal the beliefs and values of the society that created and used them. In fashion from the late 1300s to the late 1500s, these grand painted chests both reflected and helped to shape Renaissance attitudes toward a major defining moment in an individual's life.

CRAFTING A CHEST

It took many hands to create a painted *cassone*. *Cassone* painters did not sign their work, but we know some of their identities from their account books and other documents. Most famous is the account book of Apollonio di Giovanni (1415/17–1465) and Marco del Buono (1403–1480) that, along with Cennino Cennini's *Craftsman's Handbook*, gives a fascinating glimpse into the workings of *cassone* manufacture. The chest was first carved and constructed by a joiner, who would have used poplar or some fruitwood. Guild rules that governed furniture-making dictated the quality of the wood and workmanship. The unadorned chest next moved to the painter's workshop, where specialists would apply gesso to all the surfaces of the chest that were to be painted or gilded. Only the back would be left rough. Sometimes raised decorations in *pastiglia*, molded gesso, framed the painted panels (as on the Bowdoin example, which is framed with a *pastiglia* pattern of birds and buds). Decorative moldings at the foot and lip of the chest were usually gilded, as were the carved pilasters or other decorations at the outer corners. Next, using tempera, the painters added the families' coats of arms, and covered front panels with extended many-figured narratives and the side panels with one or two figures, such as heroes or personifications of virtues. The inside and outside of the lid and the rough wood of the back of the chest would receive painted patterns imitating textiles or geometric forms. Some inner lids were painted with reclining figures. Finishing touches of gold leaf or silver were applied by the gilder. Once the painting was completed, the interior of the chest was lined with fabric such as linen, silk, or even gold cloth to protect the precious possessions that it soon would hold.[1]

Notes

1 The pioneering study of *cassoni* is Paul Schubring's *Cassoni, Truhen und Truhenbilder der italienischen Frührenaissance*, 2 vols. Leipzig, 1915; Supplement, Leipzig, 1923. Ellen Callmann, *Apollonio di Giovanni* (Oxford, Clarendon Press, 1974), analyzes the artist's workshop account book. Cennino Cennini, *The Craftsman's Handbook*, translated by Daniel V. Thompson (New York, Dover Publications [1954, © 1933]), 109–110, discusses *cassone* construction. Graham Hughes, *Renaissance Cassoni: Masterpieces of Early Italian Art: Painted Marriage Chests 1400–1550* (Polegate, Sussex: Starcity Publishing; London: Art Books International, 1997), discusses prominent *cassone* painters, 174–188; and on 203–204 provides a good summary of techniques used in making a *cassone*. Callman, *Apollonio*, 26-28, discusses guild rules. John Pope-Hennessy and Keith Christiansen, *Secular Painting in 15th-Century Tuscany: Birth Trays, Cassone Panels, and Portraits* (New York: Metropolitan Museum of Art, 1980), describe *cassone* manufacture, 12. On cloth lining see Giorgio Vasari, *Le vite de' più eccellenti pittori, scultori ed architettori scritte*, 9 vols., ed. Gaetano Milanesi (Firenze, G.C. Sansoni, 1878–85]), Vol. II, 148, as cited and summarized in Hughes, 42; Ellen Callmann, *Dictionary of Art*, 1996 ed., s.v. "Cassone"; and Peter Thornton, *The Italian Renaissance Interior, 1400–1600* (New York: H. N. Abrams, 1991), 204, 383 note 44.

2 Carole Collier Frick, *Dressing Renaissance Florence: Families, Fortunes, & Fine Clothing* (Baltimore: Johns Hopkins University Press, 2002), 135. Kate Lowe, "Secular Brides and Convent Brides: Wedding Ceremonies in Italy during the Renaissance and Counter-Reformation," 48; and Trevor Dean, "Fathers and Daughters: Marriage Laws and Marriage Disputes in Bologna and Italy, 1200–1500," 100, in *Marriage in Italy: 1300–1650*, eds. Trevor Dean and K.J.P. Lowe (Cambridge, Eng.; New York: Cambridge University Press, 1998).

3 Frick, 233–237.

4 Frick, 140; Jacobus de Voragine, *The Golden Legend, Readings on the Saints*, trans. William Granger Ryan (Princeton: Princeton University Press, 1993), Vol. I, 368–370; and Jacqueline Musacchio, *The Art and Ritual of Childbirth in Renaissance Italy* (New Haven: Yale University Press, 1999), 141–142. On St. Margaret, Christiane Klapisch-Zuber, "Holy Dolls," in Klapisch-Zuber, *Women, Family, and Ritual in Renaissance Italy*, trans. Lydia G. Cochrane (Chicago: University of Chicago Press, 1985), 310–329. Jacqueline Musacchio, "Imaginative Conceptions in Renaissance Italy," in *Picturing Women in Renaissance and Baroque Italy*, eds. Geraldine A. Johnson and Sara F. Matthews-Grieco (Cambridge, Eng.; New York: Cambridge University Press, 1997), 42–60. Luke Syson and Dora Thornton, *Objects of Virtue: Art in Renaissance Italy* (Los Angeles: J. Paul Getty Museum, 2001), 61–63.

CONTENTS OF A MARRIAGE CHEST

We cannot know the original contents of the *cassoni* in this exhibition. Fortunately, descriptions of brides' trousseaux survive and help indicate what items would have been transported and ultimately stored in marriage chests. The trousseau, a collection of clothing, jewelry, and necessary household items, was assembled and paid for by the male head of the bride's family. Mothers passed down heirlooms and gifts to their daughters: linen for bed and household, clothes, and jewelry.[2] Since the most valuable parts of a bride's trousseau were considered part of the dowry she brought to her marriage, the items were inventoried and assessed.

An example of one very expensive Florentine trousseau from 1511 for Ghostanza Minerbetti is itemized in the Minerbetti family records, preserved in the Laurentian Library in Florence.[3] Ghostanza's trousseau contained exceptional garments such as gowns of pink, blue, and lemon-colored silk, trimmed with fur or velvet. Very few complete Renaissance garments have been preserved, so it is only from inventories, swatches of cloth cut from elegant garments, and the evidence from works of art that we gain a partial picture of the enormous wealth poured into a bride's clothing.

Ghostanza's trousseau also held smaller personal linens like undergarments, aprons, scarves, and handkerchiefs, which are listed as embroidered, probably worked in colored silk, silver, or gold thread. Among the special accessories that appear in the account are ribbons, little purses, housecaps, neckbands, and decorated belts. One outstanding ornament named is a white silk hairnet decorated with swan's-down. In addition to clothing there were printed books; knives decorated with silver; combs of mother of pearl, amber, jasper, and ivory; decorated vessels; a ring and mirror; and finally a little doll of St. Margaret of Antioch richly dressed in brocade and pearls. This doll of the patron saint of childbirth was passed down from mother to daughter. Women prayed to St. Margaret, who moments before her martyrdom had prayed that any woman who called upon her help during a difficult delivery would bring forth a healthy child. Such saints' dolls and child dolls (*bambini*) were intended for the bride herself, not as playthings for her children. The little dolls of children dressed in precious fabrics embroidered with pearls were sometimes specifically meant to represent the Christ Child and could be used in devotions within the household. The dolls might help prepare the bride for motherhood, since it was thought that a woman looking at a beautiful doll of an ideal child would take in through her eyes the virtues of the image. These virtues would then be impressed upon the child she would conceive.[4]

Pictures of the Christ Child and images of young children in general painted on marriage chests and birth trays could serve a similar function, such as the pair on the Raleigh birth tray (Figure 13) and the groups of playing children in the foreground of the Court of Love panel (Figure 9) in the collection of the Chazen Museum of Art.

More humble garments worked in plain linen or wool were not assessed. Neither were socks, shoes, veils, stockings, gloves, sewing supplies, and implements for spinning. Small chests and baskets finish the list along with writing supplies and a tabernacle with painted decorations of saints for private devotions.[5]

Lodovico II Gonzaga of Mantua ordered four *cassoni* for the 1477 wedding of his very young daughter Paola: two richly painted and two carved in wood and ivory showing Petrarch's six Triumphs: Love, Chastity, Death, Fame, Time, and Divinity. They are now in the Klagenfurt Museum, Millstatt, and in Graz Cathedral in Austria. Both contents and decorations of the bridal chests give evidence of the bride's education in a court center. According to an inventory of her possessions, the *cassoni* held "gold, silver, pearls, precious stones, diamonds, gowns, Arras carpets, a chess board, a wooden chest, an ivory box, two boxwood chests, ivory combs, silver knives, a salt cellar, a portrait, a naked Venus, a painted box, gilt jugs and water basin, four table dishes, plates, spoons, six small forks, table candelabra."[6]

Paola's fourteen books included works by Christian writers, among them Augustine's *De Civitate Dei* (*City of God*); works by Roman writers such as the poet Virgil, the historian Sallust, and the grammarian Donatus; Cicero's *De Senectute* (*On Old Age*) and *De Amicitia (On Friendship)*; and books by moderns: the poetry of Dante, two of Petrarch's *Triumphs*, and a work by the great humanist scholar Guarino da Verona. Presumably Cicero's two works might have come in handy for the reluctant 14-year-old Paola coerced into marrying the 36-year-old Count of Gorizia. No children from the marriage lived to adulthood, and chronically ill Paola died in 1497.[7]

Marriage chests were often ordered in pairs; the relating of two pieces may have symbolized marriage itself.[8] *Cassoni* were often richly decorated with paintings of love stories, ancient myths, heroic battles, or allegories of virtue. As Giorgio Vasari, biographer of Italian artists, wrote around 1550 when the taste for painted decoration on chests was giving way to a preference for elaborate carving:

"[C]itizens of those times used to have in their apartments great wooden chests in the form of a sarcophagus, with the covers shaped in various fashions, and there were none that did not have the said chests painted; and besides the stories that were wrought on the front and on the ends, they used to have the arms, or rather, insignia of their houses painted on the corners, and sometimes elsewhere. And the stories

5 Sara F. Matthews-Grieco, "Marriage and Sexuality," 112-113; Hugo Blake, "Everyday Objects," 340, and Elizabeth Currie, "Textiles and Clothing," 344 in *At Home in Renaissance Italy*, eds. Marta Ajmar-Wollheim and Flora Dennis, cat. ed. Elizabeth Miller (London: Victoria & Albert Museum, 2006), 112–114, 340, 344; Cristelle Baskins, *Cassone Painting, Humanism, and Gender in Early Modern Italy.* (New York: Cambridge University Press, 1998), 6.

6 Quoted in Hughes, 66, with references to the *cassoni* on 84–85; Syson and Thornton, 70; Michael Vickers, "Intended Setting of Mantegna's 'Triumph of Caesar'," *Burlington Magazine* (Vol. 120, no. 903, June 1978), 366, note 14. Michael Vickers, "The Medal of Paola Gonzaga: A Re-assessment," *Numismatic Chronicles* (1978), 144.

7 Vickers, "The Medal of Paola Gonzaga," 142-145 with reference to further bibliography. On the marriage: Exhibitions in Tyrol, "Around 1500: Leonhard and Paola, an Odd Couple" (2000); and Vienna, "Andrea Mantegna and the Bridal Chests of Paola Gonzaga (2001-2); Evelyn Welch, *Art and Society in Italy 1350–1500* (Oxford and New York: Oxford University Press, 1997), 284–285.

8 Brucia Witthoft, "Marriage Rituals and Marriage Chests in Quattrocento Florence," *Artibus et Historiae*, 5 (1982), 58, note 95.

9 Baskins's translation, 8-9 of Vasari, *Le vite*, ed. Milanesi, Vol. II, 148–149. For a slightly different translation, see Paola Tinagli, *Women in Italian Renaissance Art: Gender, Representation, Identity* (Manchester, Eng., and New York: Manchester University Press, 1997), 22.

10 Callmann, *Apollonio*, 25; Jacqueline Musacchio, "The Rape of the Sabine Women on Quattrocento Marriage-Panels," in *Marriage in Italy*, 71; Frick, 19.

11 Hughes, 30.

that were wrought on the front were for the most part fables taken from Ovid and from other poets, or rather stories related by the Greek and Latin historians, and likewise chases, jousts, tales of love, and other similar subjects, according to each man's particular pleasure." [9]

Richly decorated, often adorned with expensive gold leaf, these chests could be tremendously costly, averaging about 34 florins a pair, a year's earnings for a common workman. The most lavish examples cost as much as 60 florins, a sum that could support a family of four for an entire year.[10]

In the first decades of their popularity, the chests were part of the bride's trousseau; usually the groom or groom's family ordered a pair of them at the time of the betrothal. Later, these extremely costly pieces of furniture were simply purchased for the household by the groom, and they did not accompany the bride in her procession to her new home. Long after the custom of carrying the *cassoni* through the streets had ceased, these elaborate chests still played an essential role in the domestic life of the new couple, continually testifying to the family's wealth, taste, and prestige. They provided a locked space for valuables, while simple, flat-lidded examples could be used as extra seating, such as in the almost completely preserved *cassone* (Figure 5) in the collection of the Cincinnati Art Museum. With

planks laid across their tops, chests could provide a place to sleep (*letto a cassoni*).[11] Most important for our purposes, their imagery also gave both visual pleasure and moral instruction to the married couple.

Unfortunately, most of these massive pieces of furniture—some were seven feet long—were damaged through household use and dismantled over the centuries, leaving us with only fragments of their decorations. The Bowdoin panel is one such vestige, but one that nonetheless can offer us a window onto Italian Renaissance ideas about love, beauty, and the duties of and motives behind marriage. This essay will first recount Boccaccio's story of the *Nymphs of Fiesole* as interpreted in Bowdoin's *cassone* panel (Figures 1–4), touching on the qualities valued in a bride or groom. There follows a survey of other romantic and heroic themes found on the chests with the various meanings that these images might have offered. The essay concludes with accounts of specific individuals' marriages, illustrating how the institution of marriage served family prestige, political maneuvering, civic responsibility, and in some cases, even affection. It also touches on depictions of beliefs and values regarding marriage as portrayed on birth trays and in portraits and medals.

Figure 5:
A *cassone* with a flat lid could
be used for extra seating as well as
for storage.

Complete Cassone with Painting
of a Battle and End Panels
with Hercules and the Nemean Lion,
Hercules and Nessus, ca. 1460

Workshop of Apollonio di Giovanni
and Marco del Buono
Cincinnati Art Museum
(Checklist 2)

BOCCACCIO'S NYMPHS

One of Boccaccio's early works, the poem *Il Ninfale Fiesolano* (*The Story of the Nymphs of Fiesole*) ca. 1343, furnished the artist with a rich visual and moral theme for Bowdoin's *cassone* panel (Figure 1). Laurence Kanter, a noted scholar of early Italian art, has recently suggested that the painting dates to the very early 1400s, and hypothesized that it may have been painted by the very young Fra Angelico (active 1417–d. 1455), before he entered the Dominican order and became the most sublime painter of sacred images of his time.[12] If so, the adolescent painter, then known as Guido di Pietro, may well have been learning his art in the shop of the illustrious painter Lorenzo Monaco. Whoever the painter was who took up Boccaccio's tale of the tragic love of a mortal youth for one of the nymphs dedicated to Diana, chaste goddess of the hunt, he (and it was certainly a "he") selected essentials of the popular tale, effectively compressing the important scenes into the compact space of the Bowdoin panel.

12 On the Bowdoin panel, see Laurence B. Kanter and Pia Palladino, et al., *Fra Angelico* (New York: The Metropolitan Museum of Art; New Haven: Yale University Press, 2005), 19–21; Paul F. Watson, "Boccaccio's *Ninfale Fiesolano* in Early Florentine Cassone Painting," *Journal of the Warburg and Courtauld Institutes* 34 (1971), 331–333.

The English translations quoted in this section are from Giovanni Boccaccio, *The Nymph of Fiesole, Il Ninfale Fiesolano,* trans. Daniel J. Donno (New York: Columbia University Press, 1960).

Figure 2:
Diana warns her nymphs to beware
of men.

Scenes from Boccaccio's "Il Ninfale
Fiesolano" (Story of the Nymphs
of Fiesole) (detail)

Recently proposed attribution
to Fra Angelico (Checklist 1)

The story unfolds from left to right in a continuous land-scape marked by massive rocks and fruiting trees (Figure 2). As the poem describes, Diana is holding court for her nymphs in May among flowers and birds singing out their love. The gilded plaster relief of birds and buds that frames the painting echoes this pleasantly amorous poetic image. Eleven well-dressed young women stand attentively in front of their leader, who is enthroned on a rocky seat inside a small grotto. Diana wears a high-necked, grey-blue gown with striking yellow sleeves, with a lace collar at her throat that sets her apart from her followers. Glowing with light shown in golden lines around her face and form, she brandishes an instructor's rod in her right hand as she warns her troop, "If you happen to meet a man, …always flee from him as from an enemy, so that he will have no chance to use guile or force upon you; for I will banish and slay any one of you who is deceived" (stanza 21).

The nymphs, dressed in long flowing dresses of red, yellow, grey-blue, and pink, are all blondes with their hair bound up on their heads. The high-necked long gowns these women wear tie the action to the Renaissance viewers' world. Nymphs wearing contemporary or slightly old-fashioned garments rather than rough forest garb bridge the gap between the distant past in which the tale is set and the fifteenth-century present in which the *cassone* and its imagery function. None of the nymphs carries a bow or arrows, the standard weaponry of their kind. Only one nymph, who is standing farthest from Diana and is dressed in a red garment with low neckline and pale blue-grey sleeves, holds a lance in her left hand. Clearly not attending to Diana's instructions, she points off into the next scene in the story. Her action, her dress, and her weapon set her apart. She is Mensola, the beautiful 15-year-old heroine of the tale. She points across a gulf of space and time toward Africo, the handsome youth who is fated to fall in love with her (Figure 3).

He is asleep on a coverlet of brilliant red, the same fiery color as Mensola's robe. In fact, Africo had already appeared in the panel. On the far left, he barely peeps over a mountain crag spying on Diana and her followers. The poet describes Africo as twenty or younger, beardless, blond, with a complexion colored like a rose or a fresh apple. At his first glimpse of Mensola, Africo is hopelessly struck with love.

When we see him again in the center scene, Africo is back at the home of his mother and father. The front wall of this simple wooden structure is opened to give a view inside. Here, Africo, dressed in a blue garment and pink collar, lies in bed, his right hand propping up his head in a gesture that expresses sleep, but also melancholy. Though he has abandoned his idea of love, his urge is rekindled by a vision

Figure 3:
Mensola points; Africo sleeps; Venus encourages him.

Scenes from Boccaccio's "Il Ninfale Fiesolano" (Story of the Nymphs of Fiesole) (detail)

Recently proposed attribution to Fra Angelico (Checklist 1)

Figure 4:
Africo's parents warn him against
involvements with nymphs. Africo in
disguise seizes Mensola in the bathing
pool and the nymphs flee.

*Scenes from Boccaccio's "Il Ninfale
Fiesolano" (Story of the Nymphs
of Fiesole)* (detail)

Recently proposed attribution
to Fra Angelico (Checklist 1)

of Venus, the goddess of love. This vibrant nude figure floating in a brilliant halo of light makes a vivid contrast to Africo's mother seated below holding her distaff and spindle, spinning tools long associated with a woman's work and thus, her virtue. This image obliquely foreshadows the free-living Mensola's later refusal of a domestic life when she states that if she had wanted to spin wool with her mother, she would have remained at her father's house instead of joining Diana's band at age ten (stanza 291).

Africo, his passion reignited, sets out in his pursuit of Mensola. In the painting's next episode (Figure 4), his parents try to warn him against getting involved with nymphs, reminding him that his grandfather and two other relatives, unable to rein in their lust for the nymphs, had been killed by Diana. Still, the youth persists, eventually coming upon his beloved, who casts her spear at him before she herself falls in love at the sight of his beauty. This scene near the top right border of the panel shows just a glimpse of pink-garbed Africo and red-clad Mensola as she cocks back her arm to launch her javelin.

In Boccaccio's story, Africo cannot find Mensola again and despairs, growing thin and pale through the sufferings of love. After more help from Venus, Africo dresses as a girl and befriends the nymphs, joining them in a successful hunt of a boar. Mensola invites her new friend to disrobe and bathe with her and the rest of the nymphs, as is shown in the final image of the panel. Waiting until all of the nymphs have laid aside their weapons, undressed, and entered the water, Africo suddenly sheds his disguise and seizes the frightened Mensola, "as a famished wolf attacks a flock of lambs and snatches one and carries it away" (stanza 240). Mensola's terrified companions flee. Both Boccaccio and the painter employ the well-known poetic figure of the pursuit of love as a hunt. The sharp rocks that enclose the bathing pool evoke the cruel teeth and the threatening jaws of a wolf.

Not shown in the painting is the conclusion of the story, which may have continued onto the presumed second of a pair of chests. Boccaccio's poem describes the union of the two, how they conceive a son, how Mensola laments her transgression from fear of Diana's wrath and breaks her promise to meet Africo again. The sorrowing Africo dies; Mensola gives birth; and vengeful Diana melts her into a stream. An aged nymph carries the beautiful infant to his human grandparents, who raise him to glorious manhood.

STANDARDS OF BEHAVIOR

Fifteenth-century viewers would have viewed this painting in light of their beliefs about the physical and psychological make-up of men and women. Italian writers of advice manuals have a great deal to say about the inherent qualities of men and women and ideal modes of behavior for each. Chastity, obedience, modesty, restraint, and fecundity were the virtues expected of young women preparing for marriage. In Renaissance Italy, chastity (*honestà, castità*) did not pertain solely to virginity or celibacy. Chastity was essential for all women, whether unmarried, married, or widowed. Within marriage, chastity (*pudicizia*) encompassed purity, modesty, and faithfulness.[13] Chastity signaled restraint and moderation, and its loss held serious social consequences.

Leon Battista Alberti in his *Della Famiglia* (*On the Family*), writes in the 1430s of a husband speaking to his wife:

[N]othing is so important for yourself, so acceptable to God, so precious to me and so advantageous for our children as your chastity [*honestà*]. The woman's chastity has always been the ornament of the family; the mother's chastity has always been a part of the dowry of her daughters; chastity in any woman has always been worth more than any of her beauties.[14]

13 Leon Battista Alberti, *I libri della famiglia*, ed. G. Mancini (Florence, 1908), 209, cited in *Women in Italy, 1350–1650: Ideals and Realities: A Sourcebook*, selected, trans. and intro. by Mary Rogers and Paola Tinagli (Manchester, Eng.; New York: Manchester University Press, 2005), 25. On ideals of behavior for women and men, see Tinagli, 23–26; Ellen Callmann, *Beyond Nobility: Art for the Private Citizen in the Early Renaissance* (Allentown Art Museum, Sept. 28, 1980– Jan. 4, 1981: The Allentown Art Museum, 1980), 6; Syson and Thornton, 48.

14 Alberti, 209, cited in *Women in Italy*, 25.

20

15 Baldassare Castiglione, *The Book of the Courtier*, trans. G. Bull (Harmondsworth, Middlesex, Eng.: Penguin Books, Ltd., 1967), 241.

16 On women's nature, see Galeazzo Capra (1526) cited in *Women in Italy*, 12–13; and Scipione Mercurio, cited in *Women in Italy*, 19 and notes, discussing women's connection with water. Corresponding to the four elements that made up the universe — earth, water, fire and air — a woman was thought to be cold and moist, needing the heat of the naturally hot and dry man in order to conceive. On violence of male youth, see Matteo Palmieri, *Libro della vita civile* (Florence: Giunti, 1529) 22, and Alberti in Tinagli, 25. For other translated excerpts from Renaissance writers on women's nature and qualities, see *Women in Italy*, 12-27; and Lilian Zirpolo, "Botticelli's *Primavera*: A Lesson for the Bride," in *The Expanding Discourse: Feminism and Art History*, eds. Norma Broude and Mary D. Garrard (New York: HarperCollins, 1992), 100–109, for further translated excerpts from Renaissance writers on women's nature and qualities.

17 Callmann; *Apollonio*, 28-29; Baskins, 38-39; Musacchio, *Art and Ritual*, 132. Some scholars in informal oral statements have expressed doubt about a Renaissance date for these reclining figures.

18 David Herlihy and Christiane Klapisch-Zuber, *Tuscans and Their Families: A Study of the Florentine* catasto *of 1427* (New Haven: Yale University Press, 1985), 60–92; Musacchio, *Art and Ritual*, 77; Matthews-Grieco in *At Home*, 119.

A character in the sixteenth-century bestseller, Baldassare Castiglione's *Book of The Courtier*, says of chastity:

[I]t is wisely made the rule that women are allowed to fail in everything else, and not be blamed so long as they can devote all of their resources to preserving that one virtue of chastity; failing which there would be doubts about one's children and the bond which binds the whole world on account of blood and each man's natural love for his own offspring, would be dissolved. [15]

Men are held to a different set of standards and, in general, are seen as stronger, wiser, nobler, and more active than women. Still, adolescent males required education and paternal guidance in order to acquire the wisdom and moral probity needed to take on social responsibilities. As we have seen, Africo, ignoring his parents' wise advice, acts impulsively and violently. Matteo Palmieri, the Florentine humanist who wrote on the ideal citizen, and Alberti describe young men as headstrong and irresponsible, led by violent emotions to destructive actions and sexual abandon. One of the ways to tame these youths and bring them to sensible and moral behavior is through marriage. [16]

In a society that enshrined chastity as the principal virtue a young woman should bring to marriage, Boccaccio's nymph story may at first appear an unlikely choice to decorate a marriage chest. Mensola, deceived and overpowered by Africo, cannot keep Diana's strict law of chastity. The contest between Diana, upholder of chastity, and Venus, goddess of passion, seems to be resolved in Venus's favor. Yet it is unlikely that this emotional tale was understood solely as a cautionary tale showing the perils of injudicious behavior. There are too many seductive attractions for the viewer, from the colorful gowns of the nymphs, to Africo's inviting bed, to the bathing pool whose waters hide nothing. Both the poem and the painting proclaim the power of erotic love. And the poem, if not the painting, caps the story with the birth of a beautiful male child, the desire of every Renaissance family.

Both poem and painting overtly describe the ideal physical types of the period which presumably kindled physical attraction. The poet proclaims, "Never was such hair—so blond and beautiful—ever seen before" (stanza 273). The painting shows every figure, except Africo's grey-haired parents, with blonde tresses that are often compared to gold.

Bowdoin's panel is replete with a cluster of nude females that encourages the kind of forbidden looking demonstrated by Africo spying on Diana's band at far left. The bare nymphs in flight and Venus in her naked glory could have fed the erotic imaginations of Renaissance viewers. These nudes, and even young Africo reclining suggestively on his bed, may have functioned like the clothed or semi-clothed youths and near-naked females found in at least a dozen *cassone* lids, as in the example from the Yale University Gallery of Art's collection (Figure 6).[17] This languid figure, wearing nothing more than a garland of roses around her hips, seems to speak, gesturing out invitingly. Such inner lid paintings of reclining youths and females may have influenced those who viewed them, encouraging wedded couples toward the physical union that would bring forth beautiful children. Procreation was the central purpose of marriage, crucial in Italian centers whose populations had been drastically reduced by plague and warfare. Bearing children strengthened the civic fabric, fulfilled Biblical commands, and assured continuance of the family name, all serious duties.[18]

Figure 6:
Reclining, semi-clothed figures in *cassone* lids may have been intended for private viewing by the married couple.

Cassone Lid: A Nude Girl with Garland of Red Roses around Her Loins, ca. 1465-70

Italian (Florentine) workshop
Yale University Art Gallery
(Checklist 3)

19 On the Diana and Actaeon *desco*, see Stefanie Solum, entry on *desco da parto*, in *Encounter*, Williams College Museum of Art, ed. Vivian Patterson, et al. (Williamstown: Williams College Museum of Art, 2006); on the use of birth trays, see Musacchio, *Art and Ritual*, esp. 58–89.

20 Baskins, 26–49; Callmann, *Apollonio*, notes that the lid does not belong with the chest, 28, note 17. *Boccaccio visualizzato, Narrare per parole e per immagini fra Medioevo e Rinascimento*, ed. Vittore Branca, 3 vols. *Il Opere d'arte d'orgine italiana* (Turin: Giulio Einaudi, 1999), 213–214.

Figure 7:
The unfortunate hunter Actaeon glimpses Diana and her nymphs bathing.

Desco da parto (Birth Tray): *Story of Diana and Actaeon*, ca. 1440

Attributed to Paolo Schiavo
Williams College Museum of Art (Checklist 9)

The power of erotic suggestion is also served by the image of the bathing pool, which has been a setting for amorous intrigue in poetry and painting since ancient times. Even Old Testament stories of King David and Bathsheba and Susanna and the Elders turn on the idea of a beautiful woman spied upon at her bath by lustful males. A second painting in the exhibition from the Williams College Museum of Art (Figure 7), dating to around 1440, relates another story of bathing nymphs, this one told by the ancient Roman poet Ovid in his *Metamorphoses*, (Book 3, lines 138–243). This polygonal panel is a birth tray (*desco da parto*) created to celebrate the birth of a child. Such trays were used to bring delicacies to a new mother and subsequently became family heirlooms.[19]

The bathing scene in this painting, attributed to Paolo Schiavo, turns the tables. Diana triumphs and the male intruder becomes the prey. As Diana and her band of beauties bathe in an ornate marble basin, Actaeon, the unlucky huntsman, chances upon them. The affronted goddess splashes water on the youth, who promptly grows the antlers of a stag and is savagely attacked by his own hunting dogs. The action moves from right to left, with Actaeon shown twice, once as a fully human viewer and later after his fateful transformation. While this tray shows Diana's chaste flesh protected even from the inadvertent gaze of Actaeon, it still displays her nakedness and that of her nymphs to the viewer's eyes.

Even greater violence between men and women is depicted in a battle between Greeks and Amazons on a *cassone* from the 1460s at the Yale University Art Gallery (Figure 8).[20] Accounts of Amazons, the fiercely chaste warrior women of Scythia, abound in ancient Greek writings, but it is Boccaccio's *Teseida*, the story of the ancient Greek hero Theseus, that molds their history into a romantic tale. The first book of the epic celebrates Theseus's conquest of this nation of armed women, culminating in his taking of their queen, Hippolyta, as his wife.

On the *cassone* panel, the Greek ships land at the shores of Scythia; armored horsemen and pikemen move deliberately toward the moated and walled fortress city of Themiscyra. The armored Amazons surge across a bridge in defense of their stronghold. The powerful queen is probably the mounted warrior who clashes with the Greek hero in the center of the panel, her long golden skirts flowing back to reveal her armored limbs. The rest of her army of women, also identified by long garments, falls to the superior force of Theseus's men. At the far right several Amazons cringe away as the powerful Athenians beat them back to the gates of their city. Unfortunately, the painting from the companion *cassone* that might have continued the story has not been

Figure 8:
Theseus and his Athenians battle the
Amazons on the shores of Scythia.

Battle of Theseus and Amazons

Andrea di Giusto
Yale University Art Gallery
(Checklist 3)

21 Baskins, 26–49; Zirpolo, 105 ff.

22 Ellen Callmann, "The Growing Threat to Marital Bliss as Seen in Fifteenth-Century Florentine Painting," *Studies in Iconography* 5 (1979), 73–92; Witthoft, 53–54; John Kent Lydecker, *The Domestic Setting of the Arts in Renaissance Florence* (Ph.D. dissertation, The Johns Hopkins University, 1987), 253.

23 Callman, *Apollonio*, 62.

24 Hughes, 87.

found. However, other examples survive where the Theseus story is told on a matched pair of *cassone* panels. In these instances, the second panel shows the resolution of the battle scene: Theseus and Hippolyta as an amorous couple embarking on the voyage toward their wedding. Conflict gives way to marriage.

Art historian Cristelle Baskins's analysis of the Amazon figure in the Renaissance interprets the contest between men and women at deeper levels than the common poetic conceit of love as a battle. The chaste barbarian Amazons are violently conquered, rendered submissive, and taken from their homeland to be wed. They could be read as stand-ins for the Renaissance brides who are taken out of their fathers' homes and who arrive as "foreigners" among the families of their new husbands. As scholars Lilian Zirpolo and Baskins have shown, many marriage chests were decorated with scenes of abduction or rape. These choices align with the ideas of the Renaissance humanist Marco Antonio Altieri, whose book *Li Nuptiali* traced wedding rituals back to the ancient Romans' rape of the Sabine women, which ended in forced marriages that eventually united the two peoples.[21]

Why should battle scenes gradually supplant romantic love gardens and nymph stories found on *cassone* paintings of earlier decades, such as the Court of Love from the Chazen

(Figure 9)? Some scholars interpret this shift as a turning of attention away from the bride toward themes related to the humanistic education and interests of the groom.[22] Whatever the reality of a well-heeled Florentine merchant's life, he must have been flattered to be linked to the courage and skill of a victorious knight, such as on the front panel of the rare complete Cincinnati *cassone* (Figure 5). The upended horses, the gilded caparisons and plumed helmets, the bristling forests of lances must also have been thrilling, viewed at the eye-level of children in the household.

The same male virtues highlighted in the two battle scenes described above shine forth in the more controlled conflict of tournament combat, as shown in a ca. 1440 example (Figure 10).[23] This painting, crammed with incident, is attributed to Apollonio di Giovanni and his workshop, the same master thought to have painted the Cincinnati battle scene. Yet, this work is different. Unlike all of the other themes discussed above, this painting mirrors an actual event in Renaissance Florence rather than some mythic story. Tournaments were held in Florence to celebrate anniversaries of military victories and to mark the marriages of important citizens. One such tournament was held in 1469 to honor the upcoming wedding of Lorenzo de' Medici to Clarice Orsini.[24] It is possible that the man who commissioned the work was one of the winners of the tournament shown.

Figure 9:
The painter has added extra details
to Boccaccio's story of Filocolo. The
little children playing games in the
foreground would have been a welcome
sight to a new couple.

*Scene in a Court of Love: Filocolo's
Parable*, ca. 1425

Giovanni di Francesco Toscani
Chazen Museum of Art,
University of Wisconsin–Madison
(Checklist 4)

25 See Callmann, *Apollonio*, 42-3; Thornton, 195, quoting Savonarola as cited by Schubring, 19; quoted in Lydecker, 40, *Quam Bonus*, sermon 12.

26 Laurence Kanter, *Italian Paintings in the Museum of Fine Arts, Boston* (Boston: The Museum of Fine Arts, distributed by Northeastern University Press, 1994), 152–154, no. 40.

The crowded mass of combatants and spectators may well capture the motion, color, and confusion of the actual event. In the center background the viewing stand with the judges looms above the jousting knights. Well-dressed ladies and gentlemen look out of high windows with ornate textiles hanging over the sills. The identifiable façade of the church of Santa Croce seen on the far left locates the tournament in the open piazza in front of that building. The heraldic insigna of the Guelf faction, influential protectors of political orthodoxy, and the cross and lily of the city of Florence emblazon the doorways of the church. Tantalizing fragments of names are inscribed on the bridles of the horses that rear and mill about in the middle ground. Is "Carloto" the name of one of the contestants? Or of his steed? Colorful banners of allegories of Time and Fortune flank the scene. The richness of detail continues with the activities of Florence's more humble citizens, such as the carpenters earnestly at work on the left.

TWO NOTABLE WOMEN: A QUEEN AND A BEAUTY

The grim Dominican preacher Giovanni Savonarola, who ruled Florence in the 1490s, had no use for the vanities of fashion and idle entertainment seen in the preceding example. He harshly criticized the decoration of marriage chests, especially those with profane subjects of the loves of the pagan gods. He condemned lascivious bedroom decoration, "images of naked men and women doing indecent things," saying it corrupted children. Savonarola thought that a Christian newlywed should instead look on images that taught "the marvellous deeds of saintly women as told in the two Testaments.[25]

Savonarola, thus, might have approved of a *cassone* painting believed to have been made by the productive master Apollonio di Giovanni and his collaborator Marco del Buono sometime after 1460.[26] It presents the meeting of King Solomon and the Queen of Sheba (Figure 11), a subject found on numerous surviving *cassone* panels and birth trays from the fifteenth century. The episode of the meeting was often paired with a scene of the queen's journey to Solomon's kingdom. This gave artists great opportunity to paint exotic beasts, camels laden with chests, elaborate trappings, gilded costumes, and the queen's resplendent golden chariot.

27 Paul Watson, "The Queen of Sheba in Christian Tradition," in *Solomon and Sheba*, ed. James B. Pritchard (London: Phaidon, 1974), 116, 127.

28 Document mentioned by Julia Cartwright, *Isabella d' Este, Marchioness of Mantua, 1474-1539: A Study of the Renaissance* (New York, E.P. Dutton and Company, [1926]), Vol. 1, 15.

29 Kanter, *Italian Paintings*, 126.

The story told in I Kings 10:1–3 recounts the queen's journey to visit the king whose reputation for wisdom and magnificence had spread even to her distant kingdom. She brings expensive and rare gifts for the king, much gold, a great store of spices, precious stones, and exotic wood. In turn, Solomon answers all of the questions the queen poses to him and bestows upon her gifts from his great store of wealth. Entertained at a banquet, the queen notes the impressive meats of Solomon's table, his servants, ministers in striking clothes, and his cupbearers.

How was this Biblical story seen to relate to marriage? Bishop Isadore of Seville in the seventh century interpreted the Queen of Sheba's story as a prefiguration of the Bride of Christ, the Virgin Mary as symbol of the Christian church. Isadore compared Sheba's procession to Solomon with the journey of a bride to her husband (and medieval images show them enthroned together like Mary and Christ as the mystic Bride and Bridegroom in the Song of Solomon). Further, there is a fourteenth-century Ethiopian version of the story of the rulers' meeting that tells of their union and the birth of a son to the queen after she has returned home to her own land.[27]

Italian *cassone* painters and their clients, however, need not have known of either account in order to make a connection between the meeting of the fabulously wealthy monarchs and the rites of marriage in fifteenth-century Italy. The queen's procession through the public space of Jerusalem, the ostentatious garments, gifts, and even the monarchs' hand-clasp in the painting all resonate with Renaissance marriage practices. In acknowledging Solomon's superior wisdom, Sheba models the honor a wife owes to her husband. Such an image extolling wealth, honor, and the fruits of wisdom would surely be appropriate for a marriage. The Este family of Ferrara certainly thought so. At the celebration of Isabella d' Este's marriage to Francesco Gonzaga in 1490, the banquet hall was hung with the family's most precious tapestries showing the Queen of Sheba's visit to Solomon.[28]

In Apollonio's painting, Sheba is dressed in gold with a white veil falling to her shoulders. She joins hands with Solomon as they stand in front of a noble edifice, Solomon's temple. Like the bride and groom at a Renaissance ring ceremony they are accompanied by men and women who witness their touch.[29] To add another marital reference, little winged *putti* holding garlands stand atop the colonnades flanking Solomon's temple. This ornament follows classical models and also reminds the viewer of the power of the little naked god of love.

30 Callmann, *Beyond Nobility*, 5, no. 4.

31 On the wedding procession as triumph, Witthoft, 48–50; Callmann, *Beyond Nobility*, 5–6. For Petrarch's *Triumph of Chastity*, see Old English Books on Line: *The triumphs of love: chastitie: death*: [electronic resource] / trans. Mrs Anna Hume (Edinburgh: Printed by Evan Tyler, printer to the Kings most excellent Majestie, 1644), for example.

As demonstrated by the Sheba story, many *cassone* and marriage-related paintings praise the virtue and power of women. One comparison to the queenly procession can be found on a birth tray again attributed to Apollonio's workshop (Figure 12).[30] The tray shines with an allegorical triumphal procession: The Triumph of Chastity. As we have seen, chastity, in the sense of fidelity, purity, and modesty, was the chief virtue a married woman could possess. Here that virtue is presented according to Petrarch's poetic vision of a triumphal procession based on ancient Roman models. As mentioned above, Paola Gonzaga had two of her bridal *cassoni* decorated with Petrarchan triumphs and had Petrarch's poems in her library. Here the personification of Chastity, dressed in gold and holding the palm of victory, stands atop a golden car that looks much like Sheba's chariot in the previous example. Chastity's cart is drawn by unicorns, mythic beasts thought able to be tamed only by a chaste maiden. At the front of the chariot a blonde girl with two companions holds aloft the banner of purity, which shows a white ermine on a dark field. It was believed that the fastidious weasel would rather die than sully its fur with mud, a fitting image for a culture that valued a woman's chastity above her life.

A parade of well-dressed beauties accompanies the cart. Petrarch's poem names prominent heroines among the crowd: Lucretia, who took her life rather than live in dishonor; Penelope, who waited faithfully for her husband Odysseus for decades; and Virginia, killed by her father to save her from enslavement to a brutal, lustful tyrant. The painter of the birth tray inscribes no names, but perhaps the three women in the foreground might recall these three paragons. They walk near a little dog, a common symbol of fidelity, who laps at water from an overflowing fountain. These women and two walking close behind them carry the victor's spoils, what may be a red quiver with two sashes, and a golden unstrung bow. Petrarch states that Lucretia and Penelope tore away the quiver from Cupid's side, and the painter has included a literal representation of that metaphor. The naked god Cupid, stripped of his weapons by the noble women, is now Chastity's prisoner, bound and kneeling at the front of her cart.[31]

Figure 12:
Chastity holds Cupid captive on the front
of her triumphal cart.

Triumph of Chastity, ca. 1450–1460
Workshop of Apollonio di Giovanni
North Carolina Museum of Art
(Checklist 8)

Figure 13 (reverse of Figure 12):
Two robust, naked boys make an
auspicious image for a birth tray.

*Two nude boys with poppy capsules,
three unidentified coats-of-arms*
Workshop of Apollonio di Giovanni
North Carolina Museum of Art
(Checklist 8)

32 Apuleius, Book 4, starting on 28; Boccaccio in his *De Genealogia deorum gentilium,* Genealogy of the Gods of the Gentiles, Book 5, pp. 22 and following tells it as well, as noted by Kanter, *Italian Paintings,* cat. 50, 172; Sonia Cavicchioli, *The Tale of Cupid and Psyche: An Illustrated History,* trans. from the Italian (New York: George Braziller, 2002).

Cupid is back in action in the final example of a *cassone* painting attributed to Jacopo Sellaio (Figure 14). It treats the classical story of Psyche's love for the god of Love, Cupid, as told in a jaunty fashion by the ancient poet Apuleius in his *Metamorphoses, or The Golden Ass,* written in the second century A.D.[32] The plot involves a mortal beauty so lovely that she conquers Love himself. An accompanying theme is the severe consequence of female disobedience. Along with offering beauty, modesty, chastity, and fecundity, a wife was expected to obey her husband. Psyche's tale reinforces this lesson.

Psyche, daughter of royalty, is so stunningly beautiful that no suitor dares to ask for her hand. After consulting an oracle, her father commands her to stand upon a high precipice, where she fears she is to meet death. Venus, jealous of Psyche's beauty and acclaim, sends her son Cupid to make Psyche fall in love with a hideous man. But even Cupid himself falls beneath Psyche's spell. He has the wind gods gently bring the girl to his palace where he remains invisible to his beloved, commanding that she never try to find out his identity. Spurred on by jealous promptings from her stepsisters, Psyche sneaks into the bedroom at night with a lighted lamp and sees not a monster, but the glorious adolescent body of Cupid. Too late she regrets her disobedience. A drop of hot oil falls onto Cupid's skin and he

awakens in indignation, abandoning the faithless girl. The painter shows Psyche's futile efforts to hold onto the ankles of her departing lover as he flies off in a huff.

The panel on the second chest of the pair would have illustrated the difficult tasks that Venus set for Psyche before she could be reunited with Cupid. The fable manages to end happily with the wedding of the two lovers attended by the gods of Olympus. This cheerful conclusion to the story, however, does not mask the troubling family conflicts presented on the *cassone* panels depicting this story. Parents worry over an unmarried daughter; jealous siblings cause strife. A difficult and interfering mother-in-law-to-be (Venus) provides plenty of suffering for the future bride.

Figure 14:
Psyche's exceptional birth was probably once shown on the far left of the panel.

Story of Psyche, ca. 1490
Jacopo d'Arcangelo del Sellaio
Museum of Fine Arts, Boston
(Checklist 5)

33 For marriage ceremonies: Christiane Klapisch-Zuber, "Zacharias, or the Ousted Father: Nuptial Rites in Tuscany between Giotto and the Council of Trent," in Klapisch-Zuber, *Women, Family, and Ritual*, 178-212; Witthoft, 43–59; Trevor Dean and Kate Lowe, "Introduction: Issues in the History of Marriage," 9, 13, *Marriage in Italy*; Matthews-Grieco in *At Home*, 106–108; Frick, 115–116; and *Women in Italy*, 115–136. On age of spouses, see Klapisch-Zuber, *Women, Family, and Ritual*, 19.

34 See Stanley Chojnacki, "Nobility, Women and the State: Marriage Regulation in Venice, 1420–1535," in *Marriage in Italy*, esp. 132-139 on dowry caps; Dean and Lowe, "Introduction," *Marriage in Italy*, 11, for the Guicciardini example; Klapisch-Zuber, Chapter 10, "The Griselda Complex: Dowry and Marriage Gifts in the Quattrocento," in *Women, Family, and Ritual*, 213–246, esp. 215, 244–245; also H. Gregory, "Daughters, Dowries and the Family in Fifteenth-Century Florence," *Rinascimento* 2, 27 (1987), 215–237.

PATTERNS OF RENAISSANCE MARRIAGE RITUALS

The shape of marriage ceremonies varied widely over time and location, but one frequent pattern in Italy in the 1400s included several stages that could span many months, even a year.[33] The family first located, with the help of relatives or marriage brokers, an acceptable potential spouse for their child. Love matches between couples could receive family support, but choice of partner was firmly in the hands of male heads of families. Negotiations for a bride could start when a girl was quite young, before her teens, or even in infancy. Grooms would often be much older than their brides. In Tuscany in the 1400s the age difference averaged around eight years. Women would enter marriage by age 18, or as young as 13, while men married at 26 or even later. Over time, the age at marriage for both men and women rose, so that by 1600 the average age at marriage among elite families was 19 for women and 33 for men.

After a candidate was settled upon, the parents of the future bride and groom met privately to make an oath of agreement, symbolically sealing it with a handclasp. Though neither the bride nor groom had to be present, this was considered a formal betrothal.

The flow of presents such as jewels from the groom to his promised bride would begin after this first agreement. A second meeting of all the male members of the two families came next, this time in public. A notary was present to formalize the written contract, including the amount of the dowry, in goods and currency, that the bride's family would provide. Laws limiting dowries and laments over the crushing expense of dowering daughters crop up frequently in Renaissance records of family and civic life. The Guicciardini patriarch wanted his son's marriage to bring in a large dowry because the family needed wealth to marry off six Guicciardini daughters.[34] Even Dante in his *Paradiso* recalled the blessed days before dowry inflation:

"Nor did the daughter at her birth yet cause
Fear to her father, for her age and dowry
Had not run to excesses either way."
(*Paradiso*, XV, 103–105)

Over the following months, the groom would send expensive presents to his future wife, such as gold chains, rings, or a splendid prayer book. When the time came for the actual exchange of vows, a formal ring ceremony took place at the bride's home. The notary asked the groom and bride in turn whether they were willing to be united in marriage. They proclaimed their consent by replying "*volo*" ("I do"). The notary concluded by reciting the words, "*Quod Deus conjunxit homo non separet*" ("What God has joined together, let no man put asunder"). The groom then put a ring on the fourth finger of either of the bride's hands. According to the science of the time, it was believed that a vein connected directly from the fourth finger to the heart, thus fueling love. The ring ceremony gave further opportunities for gift giving. It was followed by a feast in the bride's home, during which the couple sometimes drank from the same vessel, another ritual of their union.[35]

It is striking that in the 1400s no priest was required to make the exchange of vows legitimate even though the words recited by the notary had been set by the Church. Nor was it necessary for the couple to hear a Holy Mass afterwards. This changed dramatically by the mid-sixteenth century after the Church Council of Trent strongly reaffirmed that marriage was a sacrament and could not be dissolved. The Church would then claim greater control over what had previously been an essentially legal and private event.[36]

However, according to the practice of the preceding centuries, the couple was considered formally united after the conclusion of the ring ceremony. Still, their actual wedding (*nozze*) had to be publicly acknowledged through further activities. Festive celebrations, including music, dance, and feasting, proclaimed the joining of the two families, announcing it to the wider community. The bride would be led in an impressive procession to her husband's home. Sometimes mounted on a white horse, she would be dressed brilliantly in expensive clothes and jewels. Porters accompanied her carrying lavish chests that held her trousseau and gifts she had received from her husband and his family. Crowds along the processional way eagerly watched this spectacle. Once the bride arrived at her new home, the private consummation of the marriage could take place, though sometimes it would already have taken place at the home of the bride. The legal contract between the families was fulfilled when the groom signed a document saying that the dowry had been paid.[37]

35 On gifts and rings: Matthews-Grieco in *At Home*, 109–110; Syson and Thornton, 63. On marriage vows: Witthoft, 45; and Emmanuel Rodocanachi, *La femme italienne avant, pendant et après la renaissance; sa vie privée et mondaine, son influence sociale* (Paris: Hachette, 1922), 59, note 2; Matthews-Grieco in *At Home*, 106–107.

36 Dean and Lowe, 6, and David D'Avray, "Marriage Ceremonies and the Church in Italy after 1215," in *Marriage in Italy*, 107–115; Klapisch-Zuber, "Zacharias," 193–196, in *Women, Family, and Ritual*.

37 Witthoft, 45–50; Lydecker, 9.

38 *The Illustrated Bartsch*, 71 Part 1 (Supplement), Isabelle de Ramaix, *Raphael Sadeler I*, (Norwalk, Conn.: Abaris Books, 2006), 269–270.

PICTURING MARRIAGE CELEBRATIONS

A highly detailed engraving of Marriage (*Nuptiae*) alludes to a number of these steps in the celebration of a marriage (Figure 15).[38] This print from the 1590s is part of a series dedicated to Duke Charles Emanuel of Savoy (1562–1630) and his wife the Infanta (Princess) Catalina Micaela (1567–1597), daughter of Philip II of Spain. It refers particularly to the benefits brought to the people through a ruler's marriage, stressing the vital duty to marry and produce a male heir to assure political continuity and stability. While the print speaks of princely unions, it still incorporates objects and activities present in more modest marriages. In the center of the image sits a splendidly dressed youth, crowned with flowers and holding a flaming torch, appropriate to Hymen, the Roman god of marriage. Surrounding him appear trappings of wealth and prestige as festivities celebrating marriage unfold. In the background at the upper left a canopied bed stands ready for the bridal pair. In the foreground, jewelry, embroidered fabrics, and a man's fancy garments spill out from an open chest and smaller coffer. A framed mirror, knotted sash, brocaded fabric, a comb, cosmetic vessels, and decorative ewer and basin allude to the elaborate adornment of the bride. Two small brooms or whisks laid out on a step beside a vase of flowers might refer to the domestic order that will serve the political order.

The scene switches from the private realm to the public as a sumptuous banquet stands ready for guests. On the right side of the image, under a columned arch graced with coats of arms of Savoy and of Castile, another banquet is already underway. Attentive servants see to the guests, and a well-stocked wine cooler stands ready at the front. In the back beyond the arch, musicians play for a line of dancers. Farther in the background crowds of spectators witness a joust and a mock combat on horseback. To the left of these chivalric displays, awed viewers point to a freestanding archway, probably an example of the elaborate temporary architecture erected to mark special occasions. Finally, a huge throng of armed horsemen and foot soldiers processes in orderly ranks before a church. They accompany their lord, who rides in front, while a splendid carriage that probably bears his noble bride follows behind. Although such enormous processions and the knightly combats shown to the right would be most appropriate for princely celebrations, they do remind us that processions through public spaces were essential elements of the fifteenth-century weddings even for the less exalted classes of merchants and bankers.

NVPTIAE·

Figure 15:
Banquets, wedding goods, tournaments, and music flank the handsome personification of Marriage.

Nuptiae (Marriage), from the series *"Schema seu speculum principum,"* 1597

Jan Sadeler I and Raphael Sadeler I after Giovanni Stradanus (Checklist 40)

Rap. Sadeler sculp.   Joan Stradan. figuravit.

Nec non tranquillam ut firmet concordia Pacem,   Se dignis primum studeat sociare Hymenæis   Hinc Princeps grata inducet spectacula turbæ,
Ciuibus et rumpat fœdera nulla dies,   Mox alijs nectat dulcia uincla tori.   Plausibus hinc populi, lætitiaq́ fremunt.

Fame, Love, and Beauty in Individual Marriages

In this last section, we examine the courtship and marriage of actual individuals whose faces we know from Renaissance portraits and whose stories are interpreted in documents of their time. Letters, poems, and biographies shed light on the characters of these men and women and on the business purposes of marriage in forging alliances and jockeying for politically prestigious connections.

Renaissance portrait medals, shown in three of the following examples, gained wide popularity in Italy by the 1440s. Worked in bronze, lead, or precious metals, they were inspired in part by the growing humanistic interest in ancient Rome. Just as the profiles and deeds of the Caesars had been preserved through coins, now the faces and accomplishments of Renaissance notables could be immortalized through medals.

Medals were struck or cast in multiples, but it is hard to gauge how many of each type were originally produced. Such durable and portable works of art were an effective means of insuring one's fame for centuries. Medals commemorated important events—the accession of a ruler, military and civic achievements, marriages and deaths. They could also celebrate an individual's learning or beauty. Given as diplomatic and personal gifts, immured in the foundations of buildings, collected for their exquisite form and invention, they recorded (and sometimes inflated) their subjects' virtues, often through allegorical figures and inscriptions.[39]

In the fifteenth and sixteenth centuries painted portraits were often used to introduce potential spouses to one another. Since beauty in a wife was greatly desired, some grooms got previews of potential mates by sending painters to the courts where they resided. In 1480 the Gonzaga family sent representatives to seek a marriage partner for 14-year-old Francesco (1466–1519) among the daughters of the Este clan, rulers of Ferrara. Their emissary reported back that five-year-old Isabella d' Este (1474–1539) was intelligent and graceful. He also sent a painting of the little girl to Mantua so that Francesco could see her face. The image and report must have been well received, because the betrothal was announced that spring. The wedding, however, was still far in the future. In August of 1484, when she was 10, Isabella

Figure 16:
Francesco Gonzaga, around age
18, presents a striking profile.

Medal of Francesco II Gonzaga
(1466–1519), fourth Marchese
of Mantua

Bartolommeo Melioli
(Checklist 24)

received the gift of a portrait medal of Francesco, possibly
Bartolommeo Melioli's bronze (Figure 16) that some scholars
date to that same year. It shows a striking curly-haired
youth, wearing a closefitting cap and elaborate armor in the
antique style. An inscription translates "the divine Francesco
Gonzaga son of the divine Federico Marchese of Mantua;
public hope and welfare renewed," and the reverse bears a
dedication to this "noble youth." Isabella did not comment
on the portrait of the "divine" Francesco. She remarked
that she would rather have seen the teenager himself, whom
she had already met.[40]

Ippolita Gonzaga (1535–1563), named for the Amazon queen,
was an exceptional woman[41] whose fame rested on more
than her marriage alliances. Daughter of Ferrante Gonzaga,
viceroy of Sicily, she was immortalized by many artists,
among them the medalist Jacopo da Trezzo (Figure 17). He
created this gentle image of the young poet Ippolita, basing
his design on an earlier and extremely refined medal made by
Leoni Leone, possibly in response to the clamor for examples
of Ippolita's portrait. In Bowdoin's example[42] of Jacopo's
medal, the girl's much-lauded loveliness is a little obscured
by the rough casting flaws. Ippolita, who was known for her
accomplishments as well as for her beauty, received high
acclaim in her lifetime, and her renown only intensified after
her untimely death.

40 Lubkin, 46; *Splendours of the
Gonzaga*, exh. cat., Nov. 4, 1981–Jan.
31,1982, Victoria & Albert Museum,
London, eds. David Chambers and Jane
Martineau (London: Victoria & Albert
Museum, 1981), 150–151. On the
painting of Isabella at age five, see the
document in Cartwright, 4; and George
Marek, *The Bed and the Throne: The Life
of Isabella d' Este* (New York : Harper &
Row, 1976), 24. On their betrothal,
Women in Italy, 124–126. On women's
portraits see Joanna Woods Marsden
in Brown, David Alan, et al., *Virtue and
Beauty: Leonardo's Ginevra de' Benci
and Renaissance Portraits of Women*
(Washington: National Gallery of Art;
Princeton: Princeton University Press,
2001), 64–87. On portraits in general,
see Syson and Thornton, 43.

41 *Dizionario biografico degli italiani*,
s.v. "Gonzaga, Ippolita," 794–796;
Splendours of the Gonzaga, 182–183.

42 Philip Attwood, *Italian Medals ca.
1530–1600 in the British Public
Collections*, Vol. 1 (London: The British
Museum Press, 2003), 105–106, 116–117;
Andrea S. Norris and Ingrid Weber,
*Medals and Plaquettes from the
Molinari Collection at Bowdoin College*
(Brunswick, Maine: [Bowdoin College
Museum of Art], 1976), 27, no. 59.

43 Aretino, *Lettere sull'arte*, ii, pp. 391 ff, quoted and translated in Attwood, Vol. 1, 105.

Married twice in her short life, Ippolita was first paired at 13 with the gallant Fabrizio Colonna (d. 1551), who had fallen in love with her from her picture alone. Ippolita lost her beloved husband only three years later. She was enshrined by Jacopo's medal shortly after her loss. Yet there is no trace of her identity as wife and widow in her garments or in the inscription on the reverse of the medal.

Rather, Jacopo's medal promotes Ippolita as the ideal of feminine beauty in an imagined version of classical dress. Diaphanous drapery pinned at her shoulder with a brooch shows off her soft throat and breast. A jewel suspended from a necklace, a row of pearls, an earring, and braided hair adorned with jewels and ribbons frame her face. Pietro Aretino, the poet and connoisseur who received one of Ippolita's portrait medals in 1552, declared that it breathed the breath of life, standard praise for a likeness. He saw in it "the sweetness of face, the strength of spirit, and excellence of manners; …not just prudence, valour and grace…but majesty."[43] He does not mention that Ippolita was also a poet and discerning judge of art, but a charming anecdote records her wit and her full awareness of the power of her beauty. In a mischievous fashion, Ippolita set up a competition between the Cremonese artist Bernardino Campi and the Florentine painter Cristofano Altissimo, charging them both to paint her portrait from life. Campi, the northerner, won out, Ippolita and her court declaring that his painting was "a better likeness, more beautiful, more

Figure 17: Seventeen-year-old Ippolita di Ferrante Gonzaga wears no mourning clothes, even though she has already been widowed.

Medal of Ippolita di Ferrante Gonzaga (1535–1563), 1551/2

Jacopo da Trezzo (Checklist 25)

Figure 18 (reverse of figure 17): Aurora, goddess of the dawn, soars over a landscape in her chariot.

Aurora in Chariot with Pegasus

Jacopo da Trezzo
(Checklist 25)

expressive, and of a better manner."[44] We also hear of Ippolita lauding Irene of Spilimbergo, one of Titian's pupils, with a sonnet praising this short-lived painter, who died at the age of nineteen. This poem, the only one of Ippolita's to survive, is included in an anthology of eulogies for Irene together with poems by the great Lodovico Dolce and Torquato Tasso. The reverse of Jacopo's medal may comment on Ippolita as poet (Figure 18). It features Aurora, goddess of the dawn, in a chariot pulled by the winged horse Pegasus, an emblem of Fame and of Poetry. Classical writers linked Pegasus with poetry and the Muses through the myth, recounted by Ovid (*Metamorphoses*, Book 5, line 256), that he struck a rock with his hoof to create the Hippocrene spring at their home on Mount Helicon. Aurora, in whose face some scholars see the face of Ippolita, carries a torch (the morning star) and scatters flowers recalling Homer's epithet of "rosy-fingered dawn." On her chariot stands a cock, whose crowing announces the start of day. The inscription reads "VIRTVTIS FORMAEQ PRAEVIA" ("pre-eminent in virtue and beauty"). Some believe this text and the image refer to the dawn of the teenaged Ippolita's talents as a poet, though only her poem for Irene of Spilimbergo has come down to us. [45]

Still in her teens, Ippolita married Antonio Caraffa, Duke of Mondragone, in 1554. Her beauty and creativity flowered for only a brief time: she died at 28.

44 On painting contest as seen in an episode from Alessandro Lamo's *Discorso intorno alla scultura e pittura*, Cremona, 1584, p. 53, cited in Robert Klein and Henri Zerner, eds., *Italian Art, 1500-160: Sources and Documents* (Englewood Cliffs, N.J., Prentice-Hall, 1966), 150–153; also letter of May 2, 1550, noted in Ilya Sandra Perlingieri, *Sofonisba Anguissola: The First Great Woman Artist of the Renaissance* (New York: Rizzoli, 1992), 48–49.

45 On Irene Spilimbergo, see Fredrika Jacobs, *Defining the Renaissance Virtuosa, Women Artists and the Language of Art History and Criticism* (Cambridge; New York: Cambridge University Press, 1997), 182; Stephen K. Scher, curator/editor, *The Currency of Fame: Portrait Medals of the Renaissance* (New York: H. N. Abrams in association with the Frick Collection, 1994), 117.

Figure 19:
The Spanish Princess
Isabella Clara Eugenia
shows off Spain's
wealth in her splendid
costume and jewelry
of pearls, gems,
enamels, and gold.

*Portrait of Infanta
Isabella Clara
Eugenia of Spain
(around age 19-22)*

After Alonso Sánchez
Coello (Checklist 12)

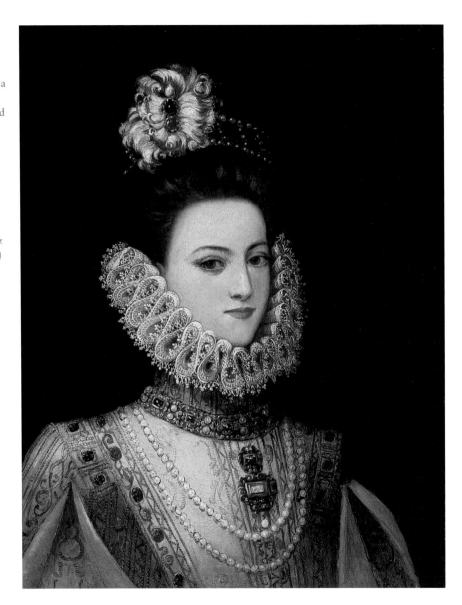

WHEN PRINCESSES MARRIED

For the Spanish Infanta Isabella Clara Eugenia (1566–1633), the cult of appearance functioned even more powerfully. The oft-painted Isabella appears in Bowdoin's charming bust-length portrait (Figure 19) in her role as highly sought marriage candidate. She was King Philip II of Spain's eldest daughter, with his third wife, Isabel of Valois. Beloved by her father, she did not marry until 1599, shortly after Philip's death in 1598.[46]

Even though she remained unmarried into her thirties, planning for Isabella's marriage began early. In 1568 when she was only two years old, arrangements were evidently put forward to link her with her cousin, Rudolf, son of the Holy Roman Emperor Maximilian II. In 1574 the idea of a marriage for Isabella with a son of the Emperor surfaced again as part of a plan to establish an independent Netherlands. Rudolf rose to become Holy Roman Emperor in 1576 and still the question of marriage with Isabella was brought up and set aside again and again.

Eventually in 1578, Catherine de' Medici, Isabella's grandmother and mother of the King of France, Henry III, suggested her youngest unmarried son, Isabella's uncle,

François, Duke of Anjou, as a possible match, but this plan, too, was rejected by Philip II. He hoped to advance Isabella's own claims to the French throne through the line of her mother, Isabel of Valois, an ambition, however, that came to naught.

Meanwhile, Emperor Rudolf II's continued reluctance eventually soured marriage negotiations. However, when a betrothal between Isabella and Rudolf's youngest brother Albert was arranged, the Emperor raged and lamented. Albert, who was at the time Archbishop of Toledo, became an archduke after Pope Clement VIII released him from his vows. The marriage then proceeded by stages in 1598 and 1599. Albert received the dowry of Spain's territory in the Netherlands, and from this point on Isabella's image showed her in northern fashions as a powerful Catholic archduchess. After Albert's death she transformed her public image to that of a pious widow.[47]

The bust-length Bowdoin painting takes us back to her earlier guise. It is a simplified and reduced version of an earlier full-length portrait of the Infanta by the painter Alfonso Sánchez Coello and his assistants. This large canvas dates to around 1585–88 and shows Isabella Clara Eugenia in her late teens or early twenties. From that majestic work smaller copies and variants were made.
The artist of the Bowdoin painting has softened the Infanta's features, sweetened her mouth into a faint smile, and shortened her nose to give it an upward tilt. Portraits were often re-fashioned or even repainted with "face-lifts" to appeal to changing tastes for female appearance over the years.[48]

Even though it is a derivative copy, the Bowdoin painting does give an impression of the resplendent costume and ornament that Isabella Clara Eugenia wore even from her infancy. Her father, King Philip II, avidly collected gemstones and owned a vast hoard of diamonds, rubies, emeralds, sapphires, and pearls. Part of that treasure ornaments his favorite daughter in this image. In the painting she wears a jaunty little black velvet hat, trimmed with pearl bands. To that is pinned a triple jewel of pearl, possibly emerald, and ruby in a gold mount set into the center of an *aigrette*, soft curling plumes of white heron feathers. At the throat of her high-necked gown she wears a close fitting collar (*carcanet*) made up of repeated blue-green stones (emeralds?) framed in red-enameled gold cartouches alternating with links set with pairs of pearls. Between the collar and two strands of pearls hangs a massive pendant: a gold-set

46 *Grove Dictionary of Art*, 1996 ed. s.v. "Habsburg I (15), Isabella Clara Eugenia." On marriage negotiations, see Henry Kamen, *Philip of Spain* (New Haven: Yale University Press, 1997), 155, 207; Magdalena S. Sánchez, *The Empress, the Queen, and the Nun: Women and Power at the Court of Philip III of Spain* (Baltimore: Johns Hopkins University Press, 1998), 118; Lili Mugnier, "Catalogue of Images of the Infanta of Spain, Isabella Clara Eugenia…" (Bowdoin College Independent Study, unpublished typescript, 2007).

47 Kamen, 303.

48 On "face lifts," Robert Simon, oral communication, 2007.

49 It is not always possible to identify the exact type of gemstone depicted. For example, diamonds were often backed with foil, a device that would mask any flaws, thus making them appear dark rather than brilliant. See Yvonne Hackenbroch, *Renaissance Jewellery* (London; Totowa, N.J.: Sotheby Parke Bernet, 1979), 46; Diana Scarisbruck, "Jewellery in Portraits by Sofonisba Angissola," in *Dedicato a Luisa Bandera Gregori, Saggi di storia dell'arte* (La scuola classica di Cremona, Annuario, Cremona, 2004), 85.

50 She had been born on the feast day of St. Clare, was named for her, was educated in the convent of the Poor Clares in Madrid, and would join the order as a childless widow. Dana Bentley-Cranch, "Catherine de Medici and Her Two Spanish Granddaughters: Iconographical Additions from a French Sixteenth-Century Book of Hours," *Gazette des beaux-arts,* Vol. 140, no. 1607, (December 2002), 314; *Grove Dictionary of Art,* 1996 ed., s.v. "Habsburg I (15) Isabella Clara Eugenia," 917.

51 On birth date: Although it is often listed as 1573, see document cited in Ronald Forsyth Millen and Robert Erich Wolf, *Heroic Deeds and Mystic Figures, A New Reading of Rubens' Life of Maria de' Medici* (Princeton: Princeton University Press, 1989), 30-31, that makes a strong case for 1575. Thus Maria would have been a youthful 19 in the Pulzone picture.

emerald (?) and what may be a huge diamond, finished with a single hanging pearl. The center oblong gem recalls Philip's famous named treasures such as the wondrous 100-carat diamond, called El Estanque or Pool.[49]

The princess's garment is sewn with yet more colored ornaments, buttons set within strands of golden cord and embroidery. On the projecting tabs at her shoulders and in bands that slant down toward her waist, the painter has added gems of blue, red and brown. These greatly simplified forms downplay what show up clearly as small jeweled crosses in the original sixteenth-century images, an essential marker of identity for the devout Catholic princess.[50]

For Maria de' Medici (1575–1642),[51] the path to the pomp of a prestigious royal marriage was a long one. Like her older relative, Isabella Clara Eugenia, she once held hope of becoming the bride of the ceaselessly vacillating Rudolf II. Maria's father Grandduke Francesco I of Tuscany had died under mysterious circumstances when Maria was a child. Her uncle Ferdinando took on the responsibility of finding an appropriate husband for her, one who would also enhance the Medicis' standing. He entertained at least half a dozen candidates before focusing on the King of France. By 1592 King Henry IV of France was considering annulling his

marriage to Margaret of Valois and marrying Maria. The king was much in need of Maria's dowry of a million *écus* of gold, but he was still deeply distracted by his court mistresses, and delayed the marriage until 1600.[52]

This painted portrait identified as that of Maria de' Medici, future queen of France, bears an inscription on the back of the chair that records the artist's name: Scipione Pulzone (before 1550–1598), and the date, 1594, but not the lady's name (Figure 20).[53] In 1594 when this portrait was made, Maria's family would still have been in the midst of (ultimately fruitless) negotiations of a marriage for her with Emperor Rudolf II, who in fact would never marry. In this clever painting within a painting, probably done for a Medici family collection, Maria is garbed in lustrous black contrasting with silver white sleeves with delicate open lacework at her throat and wrists. Restrained jewelry, just a necklace of pearl and pearl-drop earrings, completes her image. Maria looks pleasingly healthy and potentially fecund with her abdomen-enhancing fashion.

52 Among the first candidates proposed were: Alfonso d'Este, son of Ercole I, Duke of Ferrara, Modena, and Reggio; Ranuccio I Farnese, Duke of Parma and Piacenza; Emperor Rudolf II, and his supposedly violent and deformed brother, Archduke Matthias. None of these proposals went forward, and Maria herself greatly protested the idea of the Archduke as her fiancé. She, or her uncle, went on to refuse Prince de Vaudémont of Lorraine and the Duke of Braganza. Marc Smith, "Princesse de Toscane," in *Marie de Médicis et le Palais du Luxembourg*, eds. Marie-Noëlle Matuszek-Baudouin et al., (Paris: Délégation à l'action artistique de la Ville de Paris, [1991]), 50; Louis Batiffol, "Marie de Médicis," *Revue Historique 89*, Sept.-Dec. (1905), 233. Jacques Thuillier, *Rubens' Life of Marie de Medici*, text by Jacques Thuillier, catalogue and documentary history by Jacques Foucart, trans. Robert Erich Wolf (New York: H. N. Abrams [1967], 14.

53 Robert B. Simon, *From Palace and Chapel, Important Old Master Paintings* (New York: Robert Simon Fine Art, 2005), 38-41.

Figure 20: The nineteen-year-old Italian princess's red-gold hair is piled high upon her head, and she wears only simple pearl ornaments.

Portrait of Maria de' Medici, later Queen of France, 1594

Scipione Pulzone
Robert Simon Fine Art
(Checklist 13)

Figure 21:
Mother of eight children by age 28,
Archduchess Maria Maddalena
bore one child every year (save one)
in the first nine years of her
marriage.

*Portrait of Maria Maddalena of
Austria, Grand Duchess of Tuscany,
Pregnant*, 1610

Anonymous, Italian,
early 17th century
Spencer Museum of Art,
The University of Kansas
(Checklist 14)

Soon after Maria de' Medici traveled north to become
Queen of France, another Maria, Maria Maddalena of
Austria (1589–1631), journeyed down to Florence. Daughter
of Charles II, Archduke of Bavaria, and sister of the Austrian
Emperor Ferdinand II, Maria Maddalena (Figures 21 and 22)
brought the great prestige of the Habsburgs to Florence with
her marriage to Cosimo II de' Medici in 1608. Cosimo II's
father, Ferdinando I, who had orchestrated his niece's royal
marriage eight years earlier, also arranged this match.

For her proxy wedding in Graz, on September 14, 1608,
Maria Maddalena wore a black bridal dress worked with
pearls, a pearl necklace, and garlands.[54] A second ceremony
took place when she arrived in Tuscany in October. Her
triumphal entry into Florence featured many decorated
arches trumpeting her imperial connections. The wedding
procession, numerous balls, banquets, sports matches,
distribution of dowries to poor girls, acts of charity, a horse
race, theatrical displays, ballets, jousts, comedies, hunts of
game, a Solemn Mass followed by a fireworks display,
a cortège of women riders, and a spectacle on the Arno all
figured in her triumph and welcome.[55]

Figure 22:
Dupré's exquisite medal was made
at Maria de Medici's behest.

*Medal of Maria Maddalena of
Austria, Grand Duchess of Tuscany
(1589–1631)*, 1613

Guillaume Dupré
(Checklist 29)

An indication of the dramatic height to which wedding fêtes had soared is shown in the extravagant drama staged on the waters of the River Arno. Onlookers crowded the grandstands built on the shore. The watery spectacle's novelty surpassed any program that had ever been seen in Florence. It retold the story of Jason and the Golden Fleece with Jason and his allies (including the Amazon Atalanta) arriving in fantastically elaborate ships. The heroic Jason battled his foes amongst gigantic lobsters, huge dolphins, and fire-breathing water monsters.[56] At the conclusion the victorious Jason, played by the bridegroom himself, presented the Golden Fleece to the bride as a special token appropriate to her imperial family links.

Maria Maddalena's portraits show no hint of such theatrical guises despite her love for fashion. Instead, they proclaim the chief motive behind Renaissance marriage: procreation. According to Langedijk, cataloguer of Medici portraits, at least three of the dozens of portraits painted of Maria Maddalena show her as pregnant. This impressive picture from the Spencer Museum (Figure 21), dated to around 1610, may record her first pregnancy that brought forth a daughter, Cristiana. A portrait of the pregnant Maria Maddalena was sent to her sister Margherita, queen of Spain,

54 Giovanna Gaeta Bertelà, *Feste e apparati medicei da Cosimo I a Cosimo II: mostra di disegni e incisioni: catalogo*, eds. Giovanna Gaeta Bertelà and Annamaria Petrioli Tofani; intro., Giovanna Gaeta Bertelà (Florence: L.S. Olschki, 1969), 102.

55 Gaeta Bertelà, 102–127, 214–215.

56 Roy C. Strong, *Art and Power: Renaissance Festivals, 1450–1650* (Berkeley: University of California Press, 1984), 149; Christopher Hibbert, *The Rise and Fall of the House of Medici* (Harmondsworth; New York: Penguin Books, 1979), 282. *The Medici, Michelangelo, & the Art of Late Renaissance Florence*, essays by Christina Acidini, et al., (Detroit, Mich.: Yale University Press, London, in association with the Detroit Institute of Arts, 2002), 357–358.

47

57 Karla Langedijk, *The Portraits of the Medici, 15th–18th Centuries,* 2 vols. and appendix (Florence: Studio per edizioni scelte, 1981–1987), I, 175; Jo-Ann Conklin, *Crafting the Medici, Patrons and Artisans in Florence, 1537–1737* (David Winton Bell Gallery, Brown University, 1999), 36.

58 Anna Maria Testaverde, "Spectacle, Theater, and Propaganda at the Court of the Medici," in *The Medici, Michelangelo, & the Art of Late Renaissance Florence,* 126–127.

who also appears in portrait in a pronounced state of pregnancy.[57] Langedijk surmises that these portraits may have been a Habsburg tradition, one that the Habsburg brides brought to their new homes in Italy and Spain. Maria Maddalena certainly fulfilled the promise embodied in her picture. By the time this second portrait, a splendid bronze medal (Figure 22), dated to 1613, was made, the fecund Grand Duchess had already borne five children in five years of marriage.

Maria Maddalena's marriage festivities marked the highest point of ostentation ever reached in Florence, a fitting conclusion to this look at Renaissance marriage. Marriage chests may have been long out of fashion by the time of Maria Maddalena's wedding. However, her wedding festivities encompassed tournaments, mythological stories, and tales of love very much like those painted on the old furnishings. The combined wealth of the Habsburgs and Medici could not be fully displayed in just one brief passage of two decorated chests through the streets. It took weeks of public celebration with real chivalric displays, not just painted ones. And princes themselves put on the costumes of ancient heroes acting out their triumphs in extraordinary public fantasies praising the rank and power of the newlyweds.[58]

CHECKLIST OF THE EXHIBITION,
LENDERS TO THE EXHIBITION, AND
FURTHER READING

CHECKLIST OF THE EXHIBITION

Unless otherwise noted, works are in the collection of the Bowdoin College Museum of Art.

Starred (*) entries are illustrated in this exhibition catalogue. Measurements are height by width by depth.

Cassoni (Marriage Chests) and Cassone Panels

*1. Recently proposed attribution to Fra Angelico (Figures 1–4)
Italian, 1395/1400–1455
Formerly attributed to
Giovanni di Francesco Toscani
Italian (Florentine), 1370/80–1430
Scenes from Boccaccio's "Il Ninfale Fiesolano"
(Story of the Nymphs of Fiesole)
tempera on panel
11⅜ × 49¹³⁄₁₆ inches (28.9 × 126.5 cm.)
Gift of the Samuel H. Kress Foundation
1961.100.1

*2. Workshop of Apollonio di Giovanni
(Figure 5) Italian (Florentine), ca. 1416–1465
and Marco del Buono
Italian (Florentine), 1403–1480
Complete Cassone with Painting of a Battle and End Panels with Hercules and the Nemean Lion, Hercules and Nessus, ca. 1460
tempera on wood
Complete cassone: 29¼ × 76 × 29¼ inches
(74.3 × 193 × 74.3 cm.)
front panel: 15¼ × 61 inches (38.7 × 155 cm.)
end panels: 15¼ × 19½ inches
(38.7 × 49.5 cm.)
Cincinnati Art Museum
Gift of Mrs. Daniel H. Holmes in memory of Daniel H. Holmes
1933.9

*3. Anonymous (Figure 6)
Italian (Florentine) workshop
Cassone Lid: A Nude Girl with Garland of Red Roses around Her Loins, ca. 1465-70
tempera on wood
Inside of lid: 20¾ × 67 inches
(52.7 × 170.2 cm.)

Andrea di Giusto
Italian (Florentine), ca. 1400-1450
*Battle of Theseus and Amazons (Figure 8)
tempera on wood
Front panel: 19½ × 68¾ inches
(49.5 × 174.6 cm.)
Allegories
Side panel: 16⅛ × 20⅞ inches (41 × 53 cm.)
Chest: 35 × 77½ × 29 inches
(88.9 × 196.9 × 73.7 cm.)
Yale University Art Gallery
Gift of the Associates in Fine Arts
1933.61

*4. Giovanni di Francesco Toscani
(Figure 9) Italian, 1370/80–1430
Scene in a Court of Love: Filocolo's Parable,
ca. 1425
tempera and gold on wood panel
15⅜ × 48³⁄₁₆ inches (39 × 122.4 cm.)
Chazen Museum of Art,
University of Wisconsin–Madison
Gift of the Samuel H. Kress Foundation
61.4.3

*5. Jacopo d'Arcangelo del Sellaio (Figure 14)
Italian (Florentine), ca. 1441–1493
Story of Psyche, ca. 1490
tempera and oil on panel
16⁹⁄₁₆ × 59¾ inches (42.1 × 151.8 cm.)
Museum of Fine Arts, Boston
Picture Fund, 12.1049

*6. Apollonio di Giovanni (Figure 10)
Italian (Florentine), ca. 1416–1465
A Tournament in Piazza Santa Croce, ca. 1440
tempera and gold on panel
17⅞ × 60⅜ × 1½ inches
(45.4 × 153.4 × 3.8 cm.)
Yale University Art Gallery
University Purchase from James Jackson Jarves
1871.33

*7. Apollonio di Giovanni (Figure 11)
Italian (Florentine), ca. 1416–1465
and Marco del Buono
Italian (Florentine), ca. 1403–1480
Meeting of Solomon and the Queen of Sheba,
ca. 1464-65
tempera on panel
20¹¹⁄₁₆ × 73¹⁄₁₆ inches (52.6 × 185.6 cm.)
Museum of Fine Arts, Boston
Bequest of Mrs. Harriet J. Bradbury
30.495

Deschi da parto (Birth Trays)

*8. Workshop of Apollonio di Giovanni
(Figures 12 and 13)
Italian (Florentine), ca. 1416–1465
Desco da parto (Birth Tray):
Triumph of Chastity, ca. 1450-1460
Reverse: Two nude boys with poppy capsules, three unidentified coats-of-arms
tempera and gold leaf on panel
23 × 23¼ inches (58.4 × 59 cm.)
North Carolina Museum of Art
Gift of the Samuel H. Kress Foundation
60.17.23

*9. Attributed to Paolo Schiavo (Figure 7)
Italian, 1397–1478
Desco da parto (Birth Tray):
Story of Diana and Actaeon, ca. 1440
tempera on panel
27¹⁵⁄₁₆ × 27¹⁵⁄₁₆ inches (71 × 71 cm.)
Williams College Museum of Art
Bequest of Frank Jewett Mather, Jr.,
Class of 1889
62.3

Maiolica Plate

10. Maestro Domenico (or Workshop)
Italian (Venetian), 16th century
Plate with Diana and Her Nymphs,
c. 1565–70
maiolica, ceramic
1⅞ depth × 11¹⁵⁄₁₆ inches diameter
(4.8 × 30.3 cm.)
Corcoran Gallery of Art
Inv. 26.373

Portrait Paintings and Prints

11. Lavinia Fontana
Italian (Bolognese), 1552–1614
Portrait of a Noblewoman, ca. 1580
oil on canvas
45¼ × 35¼ inches (114.9 × 89.5 cm.)
Gift of Wallace and Wilhelmina Holladay
National Museum of Women in the Arts

*12. After Alonso Sánchez Coello
(Figure 19) Spanish, ca. 1531–1588
*Portrait of Infanta Isabella Clara Eugenia
of Spain (around age 19-22)*
oil on canvas
26¼ × 20½ inches (66.7 × 52.1 cm.)
Gift of Miss Susan Dwight Bliss
1948.13

*13. Scipione Pulzone (Figure 20)
Italian, ca. 1550–1598
*Portrait of Maria de' Medici, later Queen
of France*, signed and dated, 1594
oil on canvas
52½ × 38¾ inches (133.4 × 98.4 cm.)
Robert Simon Fine Art

*14. Anonymous (Figure 21)
Italian, early 17th century
*Portrait of Maria Maddalena of Austria,
Grand Duchess of Tuscany, Pregnant*, 1610
oil on canvas
76 × 45 inches (193 × 114.3 cm.)
Spencer Museum of Art, The University
of Kansas
1955.0045

15. Jan Muller
Dutch, 1571–1628
After Peter Paul Rubens
Flemish, 1577–1640
*Portrait of Isabella Clara Eugenia,
Archduchess of Austria*, 1615
engraving
16¹¹⁄₁₆ × 11⅝ inches (42.4 × 29.5 cm.)
Bequest of Miss Susan Dwight Bliss
1967.39.108

16. Lucas Emil Vorsterman
Flemish, 1595–1675
After Anthony van Dyck
Flemish, 1599–1641
*Portrait of Isabella Clara Eugenia,
Archduchess of Austria, in the Habit
of the Order of St. Clare*, 1620
engraving
6¾ × 10¼ inches (17.1 × 26 cm.)
Gift of Miss Susan Dwight Bliss
1956.24.371

17. Willem Hondius
Dutch, 1600?–1658
*Portrait of Isabella Clara Eugenia,
Archduchess of Austria, in the Habit
of the Order of St. Clare*
engraving
17¾ × 11½ inches (45.1 × 29.2 cm.)
Gift of Miss Susan Dwight Bliss
1956.24.320

18. Cristofano Allori
Italian, 1577–1621
Portrait of an Unknown Youth
oil on canvas
20¼ × 15½ inches (51.5 × 39.4 cm.)
Gift of Mr. R. P. Manson
1870.3

Bronze and Lead Portrait Medals

19. Matteo de' Pasti
Italian (Veronese), ca. 1420–1467/1468
*Sigismondo Pandolfo Malatesta (1417–1468),
Lord of Rimini and Fano*, 1446
bronze, old aftercast
1⁹⁄₁₆ inches (4 cm.) diameter
Gift of Amanda Marchesa Molinari
1966.104.2

20. Matteo de' Pasti
Italian (Veronese), ca. 1420–1467/1468
*Sigismondo Pandolfo Malatesta (1417–1468),
Lord of Rimini and Fano*
bronze, old aftercast, traces of green patina
3³⁄₁₆ inches (8.1 cm.) diameter
Gift of Amanda Marchesa Molinari
1966.106.7

21. Matteo de' Pasti
Italian (Veronese), ca. 1420–1467/1468
*Sigismondo Pandolfo Malatesta (1417–1468),
Lord of Rimini and Fano*, 1450
bronze
1⁹⁄₁₆ inches (4 cm.) diameter
Gift of Amanda Marchesa Molinari
1966.104.1

22. Giovanni Candida
Italian (Neapolitan), before 1450–after 1499
*Medal of Maximilian I of Austria (1459–
1519) and Mary of Burgundy (1457–1482)*,
after 1477
bronze, old aftercast
1¹⁵⁄₁₆ inches (4.9 cm.) diameter
Gift of Amanda Marchesa Molinari
1966.107.3

23. Gianfrancesco Enzola
Italian, active 1455–1478
*Medal of Francesco I Sforza (1401–1466)
and Galeazzo Maria Sforza (1444–1476),
fourth (1456) and fifth (1466) Dukes of Milan*
bronze
1¹¹⁄₁₆ inches (4.3 cm.) diameter
Gift of Amanda Marchesa Molinari
1966.105.2

*24. Bartolommeo Melioli (Figure 16)
Italian (Mantuan), 1448–1514
*Medal of Francesco II Gonzaga (1466–1519),
fourth Marchese of Mantua*
bronze
2¹³⁄₁₆ inches (7.1 cm.) diameter
Gift of Amanda Marchesa Molinari
1966.104.5

*25. Jacopo da Trezzo (Figures 17 and 18)
Italian (Lombard), ca. 1514–1589
*Medal of Ippolita di Ferrante Gonzaga
(1535–1563)*, 1551/2
Reverse: *Aurora in Chariot with Pegasus*
bronze
2⅝ inches (6.7 cm.) diameter
Gift of Amanda Marchesa Molinari
1966.106.16

26. Sperandio of Mantua
Italian, 1425/31–1504
*Medal of Ludovico Carbone (1435–1482)
of Ferrara, Poet*
bronze
3⅜ inches (8.5 cm.) diameter
Gift of Amanda Marchesa Molinari
1966.106.22

27. Jacopo Lixignolo
Italian, active ca. 1460
Medal of Borso d' Este, Duke of Modena and Reggio
lead
3 3/16 inches (8.1 cm.) diameter
Gift of Amanda Marchesa Molinari
1966.107.5

28. Guillaume Dupré
French, ca. 1574–1642
Medal of Francesco de' Medici (1594–1614), Brother of Cosimo II de' Medici, 1613
bronze
3 11/16 inches (9.3 cm.) diameter
Gift of Amanda Marchesa Molinari
1966.117.15

*29. Guillaume Dupré (Figure 22)
French, ca. 1574–1642
Medal of Maria Maddalena of Austria, Grand Duchess of Tuscany (1589–1631), 1613
bronze, hollow cast
3 11/16 inches (9.3 cm.) diameter
Gift of Amanda Marchesa Molinari
1966.117.36

30. Gaspare Mola
Italian (Milanese), ca. 1580–1640
Medal of Maria Maddalena of Austria as Widow, after 1621
lead
1 9/16 inches (4.0 cm.) diameter
Gift of Amanda Marchesa Molinari
1966.108.15

31. Francesco Travani, Italian, ca. 1634-1675
Medal of Ferdinand II de' Medici, Grand Duke of Tuscany, 1620, 1666
bronze
1 7/8 inches (4.7 cm.) diameter
Gift of Amanda Marchesa Molinari
1966.124.6

Monumental Furniture

32. Anonymous, Italian
Bench, second half of 16th century
with probable 19th-century restorations
carved walnut with some oak
91 1/2 × 120 × 28 inches (49.5 × 304.8 × 71 cm.)
Gift of Miss Susan Dwight Bliss
Bowdoin College

Prints

33. Unknown Artist
Triumphus Amoris (Triumph of Love), 1490
from an edition of *The Triumphs of Petrarch*,
printed in Venice
woodcut
9 3/8 × 6 5/16 inches (23.8 × 16 cm.)
Gift of David P. Becker,
Bowdoin Class of 1970
1978.12.1

34. Unknown Artist
Triumphus Castitatis (Triumph of Chastity), 1490
from an edition of *The Triumphs of Petrarch*,
printed in Venice
woodcut
9 9/16 × 6 5/16 inches (24.3 × 16 cm.)
Gift of David P. Becker,
Bowdoin Class of 1970
1978.12.2

35. Unknown Artist
Triumphus Mortis (Triumph of Death), 1490
from an edition of *The Triumphs of Petrarch*,
printed in Venice
woodcut
9 9/16 × 6 5/16 inches (24.3 × 16 cm.)
Gift of David P. Becker,
Bowdoin Class of 1970
1978.12.3

36. Unknown Artist
Triumphus Fame (Triumph of Fame), 1490
from an edition of *The Triumphs of Petrarch*,
printed in Venice
woodcut
9 9/16 × 6 5/16 inches (24.3 × 16 cm.)
Gift of David P. Becker,
Bowdoin Class of 1970
1978.12.4

37. Unknown Artist
Triumphus Temporis (Triumph of Time), 1490
from an edition of *The Triumphs of Petrarch*,
printed in Venice
woodcut
9 9/16 × 6 5/16 inches (24.3 × 16 cm.)
Gift of David P. Becker,
Bowdoin Class of 1970
1978.12.5

38. Unknown Artist
Triumphus Divinitatis (Triumph of Divinity), 1490
from an edition of *The Triumphs of Petrarch*,
printed in Venice
woodcut
9 9/16 × 6 5/16 inches (24.3 × 16 cm.)
Gift of David P. Becker,
Bowdoin Class of 1970
1978.12.6

39. Andrea Andreani
Italian, 1558/9–1629
after Andrea Mantegna
Italian, 1430/31–1506
Triumph of Caesar: The Elephants, 1598–99
chiaroscuro woodcut
14 1/2 × 14 5/8 inches (36.8 × 37.1 cm.)
Museum Purchase
1965.47

*40. Jan Sadeler I (Figure 15)
Flemish, 1550–1600?
and Raphael Sadeler I
Flemish, 1560/61–ca. 1628 or 1632
after Giovanni Stradanus
Flemish, 1523–1605
Nuptiae (Marriage), from the series
"*Schema seu speculum principum*," 1597
engraving and etching
9 1/2 × 11 7/8 inches (24.1 × 30.2 cm.)
Museum Purchase, Lloyd O. and
Marjorie Strong Coulter Fund
2006.6

Grisaille Paintings

41. Jacopo da Carrucci, called Pontormo
Italian, 1494–1556
Apollo and Daphne, ca. 1513
oil on canvas
24 3/8 × 19 1/4 inches (61.9 × 49 cm.)
Gift of the Samuel H. Kress Foundation
1961.100.9

42. Jacopo da Carrucci, called Pontormo
Italian, 1494–1556
Cupid and Apollo
oil on canvas
24 × 18⅝ inches (61 × 47.3 cm.)
Samek Art Gallery, Bucknell University
Gift of the Samuel H. Kress Foundation
K1618

Sacred Paintings

43. Pietro Orioli
Italian (Sienese), 1458–1496
St. Bernardino of Siena, after 1489
tempera grassa (oil) on panel
15 × 7⅛ inches (38.1 × 18.1 cm.)
Gift of the Samuel H. Kress Foundation
1961.100.7

44. Attributed to Francesco Francia
(Il Francia)
Italian, ca. 1450–after 1510
Madonna and Child
oil on panel
14⅛ × 12¼ inches (35.9 × 31.1 cm.)
Bequest of William H. Alexander
2003.11.34

45. Bartolomeo Ramenghi (Bagnacavallo)
Italian, 1484–1542
Madonna and Child in a Landscape
16th century
oil on panel
17 × 14 inches (43.2 × 35.6 cm.)
Anonymous loan
118.1991

Books

46. Cesare Vecellio, Italian, ca. 1521–1601
De gli habiti antichi, et moderni di diverse parti del mondo (On the Dress of the Ancients and Moderns from Various Parts of the World), Venice: Damian Zenaro, 1590
woodcuts
7¹/₁₆ inches (18 cm.), 24 pages
Rauner Special Collections Library,
Dartmouth College Library
GT509 .V4 1590

47. Anonymous, Italian, 16th century
*Horae Beatae Mariae Virginis
(Hours of the Blessed Virgin Mary)*, ca. 1520
vellum, tempera, gold
7 × 5 inches (17.8 × 12.7 cm.), 304 pages
Donated in Memory of Felix Arnold Burton,
Bowdoin College Class of 1907
George J. Mitchell Department
of Special Collections & Archives,
Bowdoin College Library

48. Andrea Alciati, Italian, 1492–1550
*Andreae Alciati Emblemata
(Emblem Book of Andrea Alciati)*,
Padua: P. Tozzium, 1621
engravings
9 inches (23 cm.), 1003 pages
Gift of Jefferson B. Fletcher, Litt. D
George J. Mitchell Department
of Special Collections & Archives,
Bowdoin College Library
N7740 .A53 1621

49. *Les fables d'Esope phrygien
(Aesop's Fables)*, trans. J. Baudoin.
Paris: Pierre Rocolet, 1638
engravings
7 inches (18 cm.), 653 pages
From the Collection of Governor James
Bowdoin II, on permanent loan from the
American Academy of Arts and Sciences
George J. Mitchell Department of
Special Collections & Archives, Bowdoin
College Library
Bowd PA3855 .F8 1638

50. Otto van Veen, Flemish, ca. 1556–1629
*Q. Horatii Flacci emblemata
(Emblems from Horace)*, Amsterdam:
Henricum Wetstenium 1684
6⁵/₁₆ inches (16 cm.), 207 pages
engravings attributed to Gijsbert van Veen
Flemish
George J. Mitchell Department
of Special Collections & Archives,
Bowdoin College Library
N7740 .V3 1684

LENDERS TO THE EXHIBITION

Chazen Museum of Art
University of Wisconsin–Madison
Madison, Wisconsin

Cincinnati Art Museum
Cincinnati, Ohio

Corcoran Gallery of Art
Washington, D.C.

George J. Mitchell Department of
Special Collections & Archives, Bowdoin
College Library, Brunswick, Maine

Museum of Fine Arts
Boston, Massachusetts

National Museum of Women in the Arts
Washington, D.C.

North Carolina Museum of Art
Raleigh, North Carolina

Rauner Special Collections Library
Dartmouth College Library
Hanover, New Hampshire

Robert Simon Fine Art
Tuxedo Park, New York

Samek Art Gallery, Bucknell University
Lewisburg, Pennsylvania

Spencer Museum of Art, The University
of Kansas, Lawrence, Kansas

Williams College Museum of Art
Williamstown, Massachusetts

Yale University Art Gallery
New Haven, Connecticut

FURTHER READING

The following is a small sampling of works readily available in English. For more sources, see the thorough bibliography in *At Home in Renaissance Italy*, listed below in the section on Renaissance Domestic Interiors.

On the Bowdoin *Cassone* Panel and Boccaccio's *Ninfale Fiesolano*

Boccaccio, Giovanni. *The Nymph of Fiesole, Il Ninfale Fiesolano*, trans. Daniel J. Donno. New York: Columbia University Press, 1960. *English translation.*

Kanter, Laurence B., and Pia Palladino, et al. *Fra Angelico*. New York: The Metropolitan Museum of Art; New Haven: Yale University Press, 2005. *Most recent discussion of panel and attribution to the young Fra Angelico.*

Watson, Paul F. "Boccaccio's *Ninfale Fiesolano* in Early Florentine Cassone Painting." *Journal of the Warburg and Courtauld Institutes* 34 (1971), 331–33. *First recognition of subject; insightful analysis and delightful description.*

On *Cassoni* and *Deschi da parto* (Wedding Chests and Birth Trays)

Baskins, Cristelle. *Cassone Painting, Humanism, and Gender in Early Modern Italy*. New York: Cambridge University Press, 1998. *Discusses cassone themes as relating to marriage and views of women.*

Callmann, Ellen. *Apollonio di Giovanni*. Oxford, Clarendon Press, 1974. *Excellent analysis of well-documented cassone workshop. Numerous black and white illustrations of cassoni and cassone panels.*

——*Beyond Nobility: Art for the Private Citizen in the Early Renaissance*. Allentown Art Museum, Sept. 28, 1980–Jan. 4, 1981: Allentown Art Museum, 1980. *Renaissance household decoration, furniture, fabrics.*

——"The Growing Threat to Marital Bliss as Seen in Fifteenth-Century Florentine Painting." *Studies in Iconography* 5 (1979), 73–92. *Analysis of changes in themes chosen for cassoni over time.*

——"Cassone." *Dictionary of Art*. 1996 ed. s.v. *Fine overview of history, types, materials of cassoni.*

Hughes, Graham. *Renaissance Cassoni: Masterpieces of Early Italian Art: Painted Marriage Chests 1400–1550*. Polegate, Sussex: Starcity Publishing; London: Art Books International, 1997. *Lavishly illustrated, readable discussion. No notes. Short bibliography.*

Musacchio, Jacqueline. *The Art and Ritual of Childbirth in Renaissance Italy*. New Haven: Yale University Press, 1999. *Discusses uses and themes of painted deschi.*

——"Imaginative Conceptions in Renaissance Italy," in *Picturing Women in Renaissance and Baroque Italy*. Cambridge, Eng.; New York: Cambridge University Press, 1997. *Beliefs about impact of images and talismans on conception and formation of child in the womb.*

On Marriage in Italy 1400–1600

Gregory, H. "Daughters, Dowries and the Family in Fifteenth-Century Florence." *Rinascimento* 2, 27 (1987) 215–37.

Dean, Trevor, and K.J.P. Lowe, eds. *Marriage in Italy: 1300–1650*. Cambridge; New York: Cambridge University Press, 1998. *Economics and trappings of weddings, laws to regulate marriage, intermarriage, and consequences of marriage for women.*

Klapisch-Zuber, Christiane. *Women, Family, and Ritual in Renaissance Italy*, trans. Lydia G. Cochrane. Chicago: University of Chicago Press, 1985. *Classic essays stemming from analysis of Florentine catasto (tax documents).*

Witthoft, Brucia. "Marriage Rituals and Marriage Chests in Quattrocento Florence." *Artibus et Historiae*, 5 (1982), 43–59. *Essential discussion of Renaissance marriage traditions and related art.*

Zirpolo, Lilian. "Botticelli's *Primavera*: A Lesson for the Bride." In *The Expanding Discourse: Feminism and Art History*, eds. Norma Broude and Mary D. Garrard. New York: HarperCollins, 1992.101–09. *Model of scholarly reading of art in context of marriage.*

On Women in Renaissance Italy

Brown, David Alan, et al. *Virtue and Beauty: Leonardo's Ginevra de' Benci and Renaissance Portraits of Women*. Washington: National Gallery of Art; Princeton: Princeton University Press, 2001. *Portraits of women; beliefs about women; beautifully illustrated in color.*

Hutson, Loma, ed. *Feminism and Renaissance Studies*. Oxford; New York: Oxford University Press, 1999. *Essays on women in Renaissance economy, sexuality, dowries, literature.*

Johnson, Geraldine A., and Sara F. Matthews-Grieco, eds. *Picturing Women in Renaissance and Baroque Italy*. Cambridge, Eng.; New York: Cambridge University Press, 1997.

Tinagli, Paola. *Women in Italian Renaissance Art: Gender, Representation, Identity*. Manchester, Eng., and New York: Manchester University Press, 1997.
Excellent general introduction to images of women, society, art forms.

Women in Italy, 1350–1650: Ideals and Realities: A Sourcebook. Selected, trans. and intro. by Mary Rogers and Paola Tinagli. Manchester, Eng.; New York: Manchester University Press; New York, 2005.
Translations of short selections from Renaissance documents discussing women.

On Renaissance Domestic Interiors

At Home in Renaissance Italy, eds. Marta Ajmar-Wollheim and Flora Dennis; cat. ed. Elizabeth Miller. London: Victoria & Albert Museum, 2006.
Voluminous exhibition catalogue focused on Florence and Venice.

Syson, Luke, and Dora Thornton. *Objects of Virtue: Art in Renaissance Italy*. Los Angeles: J. Paul Getty Museum, 2001.
Household decoration and art's use in daily life.

Thornton, Peter. *The Italian Renaissance Interior, 1400–1600*. New York: H.N. Abrams, 1991.
Essential study of forms, uses, materials and terminology. Makes available J. K. Lydecker's excellent scholarship from his thesis and Italian publication.

On Renaissance Festivals

Mylryne, J. R., Helen Watanabe-O'Kelly, and Margaret Shewring, eds. *Europa Triumphans: Court and Civic Festivals in Early Modern Europe*, 2 vols. Hampshire, Eng.; Burlington, Vt.: Ashgate, 2004.
Public art celebrating noble marriages.

Strong, Roy C. *Art and Power: Renaissance Festivals, 1450–1650*. Berkeley, Calif.: University of California Press, 1984.
Examples of extravagant use of visual art in princely spectacles.

On Renaissance Medals

Attwood, Philip. *Italian Medals 1530–1600 in British Public Collections*. London: The British Museum Press, 2003.
New scholarship on distinguished collections of medals.

Chambers, David, and Jane Martineau, eds. *Splendours of the Gonzaga*. London: The Victoria & Albert Museum, 1981.
Portrait medals in context of family patronage.

Norris, Andrea S., and Ingrid Weber. *Medals and Plaquettes from the Molinari Collection at Bowdoin College*. Brunswick, Maine: Bowdoin College, 1976.
Original publication of Bowdoin's medals; see newer scholarship for additional information.

Scher, Stephen K., ed. *The Currency of Fame: Portrait Medals of the Renaissance*. New York: H. N. Abrams in association with the Frick Collection, 1994.
Splendidly illustrated in color; thorough scholarly discussion of culture of medal production, individual sitters, and craftsmen.

On Costume and Jewelry

Conklin, Jo-Ann. *Crafting the Medici, Patrons and Artisans in Florence, 1537–1737*. David Winton Bell Gallery, Brown University, 1999.
Detailed discussion of Medici dress and adornment in Uffizi portraits.

Frick, Carole Collier. *Dressing Renaissance Florence: Families, Fortunes, & Fine Clothing*. Baltimore: Johns Hopkins University Press, 2002.
Superb analysis of documents on fabrics, form, and costs of wedding clothes.

On the Medici

Langedijk, Karla. *The Portraits of the Medici, 15th–18th Centuries*, 2 vols. and appendix. Florence: Studio per edizioni scelte, 1981–1987.
Masterful catalogue of Medici portraits, surviving and lost, in all media. Hundreds of black and white images.

The Medici, Michelangelo, & the Art of Late Renaissance Florence, essays by Christina Acidini [et al.]. Detroit, Mich.: Yale University Press, London, in association with the Detroit Institute of Arts, 2002.

For images and information on the Renaissance paintings, medals and prints in the Bowdoin College Museum of Art online please go to: www.bowdoin.edu/art-museum

Cover illustration (detail):
Recently proposed attribution
to Fra Angelico
Italian, 1395/1400–1455
Formerly attributed to
Giovanni di Francesco Toscani
Italian (Florentine), 1370/80–1430
Scenes from Boccaccio's
"Il Ninfale Fiesolano"
(Story of the Nymphs of Fiesole)
tempera on panel
Gift of the Samuel H. Kress
Foundation
Bowdoin College Museum of Art

Catalogue designed by Judy Kohn
Chicago, Illinois

Printed by Kirkwood Printing
Wilmington, Massachusetts